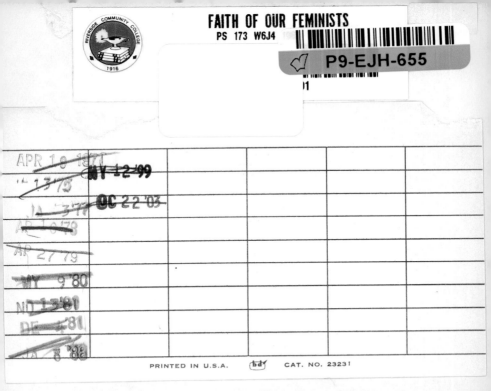

THE FAITH
OF OUR
FEMINISTS

THE FAITH

OF OUR

FEMINISTS

A Study in the Novels of
EDITH WHARTON, ELLEN GLASGOW, WILLA CATHER

By

JOSEPHINE LURIE JESSUP

BIBLO and TANNEN
NEW YORK
1965

Reprinted, 1965, with the permission of

Richard R. Smith by

Biblo and Tannen Booksellers and Publishers, Inc.

63 Fourth Avenue   New York, N.Y. 10003

Library of Congress Catalog Card Number: 65-23482

Printed in U.S.A. by
NOBLE OFFSET PRINTERS, INC.
NEW YORK 3, N. Y.

To

MY MOTHER AND MY HUSBAND

My acknowledgments to

Dr. Richmond Croom Beatty, for his courtesy as first reader;

Dr. Edgar Hill Duncan, Jr., whose patience as second reader far exceeded the line of duty;

Dr. Walter Clyde Curry, for his faith and encouragement over the years;

Mr. Raymond Leslie Goldman, who taught me whatever I know about literary form.

Josephine Lurie Jessup.

Nashville, Tennessee, 1949.

CONTENTS

I

THE CULT AND ITS VOTARIES

FEMINISM is probably as old as the awareness of sex. Straightway woman discovered her limitation, she set about denying it. The vehemence of her denial is embedded in myth. Athena not only managed without a husband, she scarcely acknowledged a father. For all Homer's mention of a contrary fact, the virgin goddess was self-engendered; and few poets have doubted that she transacted the business of immortality as an independent Olympian.

On the mortal plane the prowess of disjoined femininity found repeated classical expression. The autonomy of the Amazons was as well established as the might of Achilles; the Lemnian women, even to Hypsipyle, rose from the murder of their husbands without regret; and among the Danaids only Hypermnestra demurred at widowhood.

If the Amazon, the Lemnian, the Danaid, tends to disappear in the mists of prehistory, the Roman vestal offers documented challenge to the dominion of Cupid. Desiring neither marriage nor the *manus* of a masculine relative, the religious celibate enjoyed detached existence, buying and selling property at will, attending processions when she would, going about her affairs with a freedom which exceeded that of the Augusta.

The advantages of the Vestal's state did not escape early Christian women. With only a distant preceptor to remind them of bisexual creation, abbesses, prioresses, and their dedicated subordinates bore ecclesiastical witness to the independence of women. Mediaeval feminism likewise expressed itself outside the convent, in the secular *beguinage,* where, despite the interference of masculine guilds, women demonstrated their ability to live without men.

If the witch be excluded as too anomalous for the purview of feminism and the female hermit as too rare, mediaeval patterns appear to have suffered slight alteration in modern times. The convent continues under its own name, the secular establishment finds a dozen others. Indeed, a historian might search long before finding an era more favorable to feminism than the American twentieth century. Between the *beguinage* and the modern professional clubhouse lies the mechanical revolution, than which no other circumstance has more richly enhanced the prestige of Athena.

The celebration of this prestige has occupied novelists for at least fifty years. Unlike sociologists and other tractarians, writers of fiction have recognized feminism as lying deeper than the demand for economic opportunity or political enfranchisement. As it appears in modern fiction, feminism is an expression of woman's desire "to be herself"; that is, to measure attainment irrespective of sexual function. With a tradition continuously in force since the beginning of consecrated celibacy and a scope vastly extended by science, invention, and democratic custom, the feminist has provided a heroine for innumerable writers.

Not a few of these writers have been men. Henry Kitchell Webster in *The Real Adventure,* Booth Tarkington in *Alice Adams,* Charles Caldwell Dobie in *Less than Kin* (to name but an example by each author), all sing of non-sexual achievement and a woman.   But more often feminism has engaged members of its own sex, and none more successfully than Edith Wharton, Ellen Glasgow, and Willa Cather.

No sooner is this trio singled out than a host of rivals demand consideration.   Gertrude Atherton, for example.   According to European estimates in the 'nineties, Mrs. Atherton outranked all other novelists in the United States; and in her own country half a century later she still held place, if only by the exuberance of her output.   Producing a novel annually, she was able to exploit the fictional possibilities of reincarnation, dipsomania, gland transference; of local politics and foreign relations; of Periclean Athens and pioneer California.   And always her protagonist was a woman.

X But after this writer has been credited with energy, inventiveness, and columnist's scent for the topical, the balance begins to weigh against her.   Mrs. Atherton's method is hasty and garish, in the fashioning alike of sentences and plots; her characterization meets only the demands of melodrama; and although pursued without let, her feminism impresses the reader neither by its acerbity nor by its passion.

Equally committed to the glorification of her own sex, but in a manner different from Mrs. Atherton's, was Elizabeth Madox Roberts.   Abroad, Miss Roberts ranked as peerless among American contemporaries; at home she was set beside the best of European writers. That Miss Roberts' work bespeaks high sincerity and a poet's feeling for language cannot be denied.   To read *The Time of Man* is to walk in the pastures of the Psalmist—although never with his serenity.   For, throughout the writings of Miss Roberts, there is a pervasive hopelessness, a buckling of the spirit beneath the burden of life.   Words seem a defense against the pain of vision; characters move mistily behind a veil; and although in this shadowland woman achieves an independent triumph as complete as Ellen Chesser's, the feminism of Elizabeth Madox Roberts belongs more properly to reverie than to the literature of conflict.

Another novelist who cannot be disregarded is Pearl Buck, the first American woman to receive the Nobel prize. As a feminist rating of the sexes, few books are more explicit than *The Good Earth*. The title itself salutes the heroine. A Chinese wife who was once a slave, O-lan personifies every attribute ordinarily ascribed to Nature: patience, thrift, wisdom, fertility. From O-lan, as from earth, come all treasures; not children merely, but coins and jewels. Like earth, woman endures. Neither man's ravishing nor his abandonment affects her. He will pass away; it is she who survives, in death as in life. Man's transience as against woman's enduring worth receives telling preachment in *The Good Earth*.

Yet when this book has been praised, and praised to the full, not only for characterization, but for style, narrative structure, and authenticity of background, its uniqueness unsettles the author's claims as a novelist of extent. With *The Good Earth*, Mrs. Buck appears to have spent her substance as a creator of fiction in the large. The remainder of her novels reveal either an interest frankly commercial or a scant residue of material over that already consumed by the work which established the reputation of Pearl Buck.

For a study of feminism in relation to the American novel, Edith Wharton, Ellen Glasgow, and Willa Cather offer not only a full list of titles but a singularly uniform standard of workmanship. Although late in life Edith Wharton made concessions to the slick page, she wrote enough serious fiction to warrant detailed and respectful analysis. Throughout the publication of twenty novels, Ellen Glasgow kept free of serializing entanglements; she never so much as entered a competition; and seldom did she permit a topical event to divert her from the long view of the human adventure. Unlike commercial writers with similar themes, Willa Cather sought in pioneer America only that profit which accrues to an artist searching for truth.

Grouped together because of their probity, Edith Wharton, Ellen Glasgow, and Willa Cather show other similarities. Each lived beyond the age of seventy, devoting ripened powers to a vocation which had absorbed her from youth. All three traced descent from ancestors who had been Americans for generations. All three shared the influence of Anglicanism as a shaping faith. But, most important for this study, Edith Wharton, Ellen Glasgow, and Willa Cather testify to an engrossing feminism. The only one of the three novelists to marry, Edith Wharton divorced her husband after a separation of many years. Ellen Glasgow identified herself not only with the suffragist but with the whole woman's movement. Willa Cather declared her admiration for big characters and big careers, especially when they were the characters and careers of women. And the spirit of her whom these writers zealously served—Athena, the spirit of woman disjunct and triumphant in her separateness—shows forth in the body of their novels.

II

EDITH WHARTON

Drawing-Room Devotee

SELDOM has a writer undertaken the enthrone-
ment of her sex with firmer consistency than Edith
Wharton. For the space of twenty novels she attempts
to show woman preëminent, man trailing at heel. *The
Buccaneers,* a posthumous fragment appearing in 1937,
declares the same intention as *The Valley of Decision,*
published in 1902.

Mrs. Wharton's first novel is, however, no raucous
preachment of feminism. A high-bred lady in literature as in life, the author pays genteel homage to
Athena. Writing with a grace given to few American
stylists, Edith Wharton has in *The Valley of Decision*
recalled for many readers the measured wisdom of
Marius the Epicurean. The story of Odo Valsecca,
reigning duke of Pianura, shows Mrs. Wharton at
home and at ease in the eighteenth century. Matthew
Arnold has said that a person writes best of his own
time; and that statement is true, provided the critic
recognize spiritual contemporaneity. Edith Wharton's
own time is the century of Mozart and Chippendale, a
century which still recognized aristocratic values.
Democracy's challenge of these values aggravated the
young duke's predicament.

But the character of Odo Valsecca is shaped less
by the *zeitgeist* than by women. From women he
learns humility; they teach him little else. His foster-

14

mother, Filomena, rations out hard bread and cast-off peasant clothing; his real mother, after years of absence, squirms free of his muddy embrace. Countess Clarice receives his wild flowers with contempt. The widow of his late cousin marries him out of hand. And always Fulvia Vivaldi proves him her manipulated creature.

Living on in the cause for which her father has died, the cause of popular government, Fulvia persuades Odo to renounce love in favor of a throne. She is the zealot of the piece; he, the vaguely sympathizing spectator. Indeed, Fulvia may be taken as the feminist heroine *par excellence,* a woman who dies not in childbirth nor in defense of her honor but on the way home from an academic occasion! The professor's daughter has been supporting her doctoral thesis before a board of examiners, her royal lover looking on, while outside the scholarly hall the mob gathers violence. The bullet intended for Duke Odo lodges in the body of Fulvia Vivaldi.

With *The Valley of Decision,* her first novel, Edith Wharton announces the sexual pattern which her fiction will follow during more than three decades. The woman will rise above the man so as to stand almost in relation of goddess to mortal, sufficient in her own right, but bending down because of human need. Such is the case with the last novel Mrs. Wharton lived to finish (*The Buccaneers* was left incomplete at her death). Like *The Valley of Decision,* this story also occupies two volumes, each however bearing its own title, *Hudson River Bracketed* (1929) and *The Gods Arrive* (1932). Out of her own faith in the hero, the author tries to persuade her readers that Vance Weston's literary gifts, although unevenly and sporadically manifested, are worth the devotion of two women. But how good a novelist Vance Weston eventually proves himself is conjectural; whereas the courage with which Laura Lou Weston lives out her boarding-house days, the unnoticed wife of a celebrity, and dies of tuberculosis, induced by her husband's folly, is compassionately documented. Neither does Mrs. Wharton skimp delineation of the other woman who dedicates herself to Vance Weston's alleged genius. Like Fulvia Vivaldi, the first heroine from Mrs. Wharton's pen, Heloise Spear is another frequenter of libraries; and again, like her earlier Italian prototype, Heloise not only exerts herself to enlarge her lover-pupil's mind but buffets convention to become his mistress. The voluntary immolation of both wife and mistress emphasizes the unworthiness of the man they serve. Thus, at the close of her literary endeavor, as at the beginning, Edith Wharton assigns the real gains of character to women. The men, fickle in love and wavering in purpose, show only a steadfast puerility.

2

Within the limits set by her first novel and the last which the author lived to complete, Mrs. Wharton's feminism finds channels of varying effectiveness. While none of her fiction lacks implicit statement of the anti-masculinist position, many stories sputter without fire. The group under immediate consideration will deal with novels in which, for one reason or another, the duel between the sexes results in no significant victory.

Such a novel is *The Fruit of the Tree* (1907). Swerving from the customary social orbit of Mrs. Wharton's fiction, this story nevertheless maintains a consistent sexual paradigm. John Amherst, bent on repulsing commercial exploitation, seems an anachronistic Adam less because of his factory background and Miltonic evaluation of the sexes, than because of his apparent ignorance of the Fall as applied to himself. From so Pharisaic a hero, the reader turns in haste to Amherst's first wife, Bessie Westmore, who prefers society to social uplift, and to her successor, Justine Brent, who does not scruple at murder.

Scarcely more interesting is the hero of *Madame de Treymes*, a novelette which appeared during the same year as *The Fruit of the Tree* (1907). John Durham was called forth by literary exigency. Without a man there could have been no plot; certainly not this plot, with its contrast of French and American mores. Whatever the qualities of Madame de Treymes (and they will appear differently, the author implies, whether the appraiser be French or American), they belong to a vital being. Less can be said of John Durham, who stands for American integrity and fair dealing—stands straight as a tailor's dummy.

In search of a feminist vehicle, Edith Wharton often settled upon a French background, and seldom to effective purpose. Both staged in France, her war novels are weak performances, the result not only of expatriate authorship but of basically uncongenial theme. Despite her love for France and her convictions as to the identity of the villain in World War I, she was unable to contrive for *The Marne* (1918) a better protagonist than Troy Bellknap, who deviates in no way from the standard war-struck boy who swamps magazine fiction whenever patriotism becomes a high fashion. Mrs. Wharton's second attempt at dealing with military dissension is but slightly more successful. Seeking to portray paternal love sublimated into a larger patriotism, *A Son at the Front* (1923) outlines a theme beyond the reach of its characters. The boy remains a dim and, finally, a dead St. George; the father, a portrait painter who has left wife and child

to adventure with a girl glimpsed through a train window, seems the victim of a spiteful feminist, who
punishes her principal masculine character by killing
off the son he has earlier abandoned.

If the delicately modulated voice of Edith
Wharton is lost in the clangor of battle, it often fails
to discover an effective sounding-board in times of
peace. *The Age of Innocence*, Pulitzer prize-winner
for 1920, marks such a failure. And this is strange,
since both theme and setting appear ideally suited
to the purposes of a drawing-room feminist. But
Newland Archer is too patently of straw to be dragged
in a triumph. Even a drawing-room adversary would
find little zest in binding to the wheels of her limousine
a creature whom mothers, aunts, grandmothers, and
long-dead ancestresses have shaped into the proper
likeness of husband. Archer's complete pliability in
the hands of women, on earth and in the grave, forms
too weak a contrast for the daring of the Countess
Olenska. In a society which raises every ,barrier
against a woman living apart from her husband, the
Countess faces the censure of two continents, sustained
only by her own good conscience. The story of Ellen
Olenska and Newland Archer depicts not star-crossed
love nor even the subdual of masculine lust by feminine
chastity. What *The Age of Innocence* actually concerns itself with is the bleating of a pusillanimous
mortal after a divinity, and by such concern looks
toward the realm of metaphysics, outside the tough
province of the novel.

A less disparate situation is formed by Susan and
Nick Lansing in *The Glimpses of the Moon* (1922).
Beginning the story as a social hanger-on, Susan learns
the sweet uses of adversity in time to teach her husband, and in time to proclaim a feminist victory for a

book which through several chapters appeared to be endowing the hero with superior character. But *The Glimpses of the Moon* is a slick magazine piece, not seriously calculated to forward the anti-masculinist position.

Neither is the cause of feminism measurably advanced by the first and third novelettes grouped under the general title of *Old New York* (1924), a series which seems to stem from the author's richest material. Search for an epitome of Edith Wharton's methods and craftsmanship might profitably lead to *False Dawn*, the first story in *Old New York*. Here is a miniature of all the excellences which characterize an author who was twice an aristocrat, by birth and by vocation. But the common touch, which binds all women in a struggle against the male, is well-nigh absent. A critique upon changing aesthetic taste, *False Dawn* provides Mrs. Wharton a lame carriage. She whips up the horses with a fine gloved hand, until bystanders become exercised over the tyrannous Mr. Raycie. How the man cows every female within shouting range—and he living on the dowry of his wife! But the brunt of Raycie's despotism falls upon his son, who, commissioned to buy pictures after the school of Raphael, returns with a batch of Italian Primitives. Here, obviously, is scant material for the feminist. Mrs. Wharton does the best she can, but the result hovers insipidly between art criticism and a personified tract upon human stupidity. The bluntness of the average understanding again occupies the author in *The Spark*, the third novelette of *Old New York;* in considering Hayley Delane's failure to appreciate the poetry of Walt Whitman, Mrs. Wharton finds an even less congenial theme than in *False Dawn*. The second and fourth novelettes of *Old New York* are among the

author's most successful statements of the feminist
position, and as such will be considered in another
section.

Meanwhile, there remain *Twilight Sleep* (1927)
and *The Children* (1928). In the former, Dexter
Manford, an energetic self-made lawyer from the
Middle West bids for a stronger initial appeal than
any other masculine character of the author's contriv-
ing. But when Manford attempts simultaneous affairs
with a middle-aged married woman and his own step-
daughter-in-law, he rapidly loses place to his wife.
Pauline Manford, however, graves few lines upon the
feminist pattern, or upon any other. A congenital
groper, she acts out the title of *Twilight Sleep*, mud-
dling the anti-masculinist message through the inadequacy of her own character.

The failure of *The Children* as a feminist vehicle
can hardly be counted against its heroine. Almost
alone in a novel which uses luxury liners and resort
hotels to point up the folly of epicureanism, Rose
Sellars preserves both good humor and good sense.
Certainly she stands superior to her bolting fiancé,
Martin Boyne; as Judith, the eldest of the children,
rises above this same middle-aged man, who can not
distinguish between paternal and erotic sentiment. The
victory of womankind over man is complete enough
in this novel; too complete, perhaps, turning the reader
toward conflicts more skillfully weighted on the side
of feminism.

But even in this catalogue of comparative failures
can be discerned the integrity of Edith Wharton. No
matter how weakly elaborated, her essential thesis
remains: man is the lesser woman. The novels to be
discussed in the following section enunciate this preachment with passion and often with power.

3

In her first novel, *The Valley of Decision* (1902),
and in *The Gods Arrive* (1932), the last to be completed, Edith Wharton chose as principal masculine
character a man whose essential puerility unfitted him
for the mature business of life. But in those books
which earned her contemporary international hearing
and which, posthumously, echo the strongest tones of
her living voice, the hero's role is occupied by a man of
full stature. Only such a man is worth a feminist's
weapons. That Athena overmastered Ganymede
would not prove suzerainity; to establish her demesne
she must engage an Olympian of her own rank, of a
superior rank, Zeus himself perhaps. Those novels
which display the basic virtue of Edith Wharton, her
raison d'être as a writer, contain masculine portraits
which the critic Edmund Wilson has identified as of
men set apart from their neighbors by education, sensi-
bility, and intelligence.

The House of Mirth (1905) contains a hero of
this type. When the book opens, Lawrence Selden
has been practicing law for a number of years; has
broken with a married woman who violently wishes
to continue as his mistress; and has established himself, slight shabbiness and bookish tastes notwithstanding, as a bachelor well-adapted to house-parties
and dining out. Lily Bart, the woman of the story, unmarried and penniless at twenty-nine, claims no profession; she has not waived convention, except for an
innocent visit to Selden's apartment; nor is she tol-
erated by the rich except as an unpaid, ungossiped-
about social secretary, with clothes above reproach.
Fond of cards and dancing, lacking the will to remove
herself from parasitic dependency, and yet unwilling
to clinch an expedient husband, Lily Bart presents

herself as no strong character.   For sobriety and cool
judgment Lawrence Selden offers an ideal foil.   But, as
is consistent with feminist composition, he remains a
foil throughout the long book, the black broadcloth
necessary to set off the iridescence of a woman's evening
gown.   Lily Bart is the life of the novel; Lawrence
Selden happens to be the man who intermittently
appoints himself to save her from destruction by a
frivolous society.   He does not save her; he does not
even help her to save herself.   Lily Bart finds her own
way; and if that way fails to trace out a successful
life, it leads to an honorable death.

No less decisive is the feminist victory celebrated in
Ethan Frome (1911).   For several decades literary
fashion has rested the whole of Edith Wharton's reputation on this volume, simultaneously praising its
craftsmanship and denying that the craft was put to
any good use.   A sense of social superiority prevented
the author from drawing near her poverty-bitten New
Englanders, first in *Ethan Frome* and later in *Summer,*
critics allege.   During her own lifetime, Mrs. Wharton
came to the defense of her own pre-Tobacco Road
realism by asserting that details of the freebooting
colony depicted in *Summer* had been supplied by her
rector.   Now, undoubtedly, it is one thing to learn
about a certain class from one's rector, and another to
abide with that class spiritually.   But too much must
not be made of Mrs. Wharton as the Lady of Lenox,
dweller on the Mount; she descended into both rural
and urban slums with generous understanding.   Examination of *Ethan Frome* and *Summer* will show that
Mrs. Wharton does not condemn her characters because they are socially ill-placed.   Charity Royall, of
illegitimate birth and herself an unmarried expectant
mother, understands how to cope with fate; Ethan

Frome, a poor farmer, does not. What the author has
to say, in the short pieces of New England indigence
as well as in the longer works dealing with the luxury
of Mayfair and Faubourg St. Germain, is that woman
exceeds man.

Mrs. Wharton's convictions regarding the sexes
never find more economical statement than in *Ethan
Frome*. The name character is well individualized; it
is the women who "play opposite" him, the one indistinguishable from the other in the querulousness of old
age. But Ethan can remember his wife, Zenobia, as
youngish, though his senior, and Mattie Silver as
hardly more than a girl. About his marriage Ethan
has had little to say; but even before Zenobia makes
him her husband, he knows the feel of the tether. Life
has a habit of stomping on his wishes, whether they
shape themselves into ambition for an engineering education or for success as a farmer. And his desire for
love is treated even more harshly. Fate permits him
neither money for elopement nor skill sufficient to
bring off a double suicide. *Ethan Frome* describes an
acute case of frustration, but frustration for Ethan
alone; the women manage to have their own way, if
only to the extent of ordering about one man between them.

Summer brings about feminine triumph upon a
more felicitous level. Again, as in the case of *Ethan
Frome*, no failure of portraiture causes the men of
Summer to recede before the claims of the girl. The
aging lawyer, Royall, is well enough drawn, what
with lechery, cruel temper, and open-handedness com-
bining to form a plausible delineation of human character. As for the young architect, Harney, his near-
sightedness, soft palms, and knack of sketching old
houses, furnish excellent identification. Another story

might have provided Royall a sympathetic place; but in a novelette appropriately called *Summer*, his years only underline the plight of his young ward, Charity. Lucius Harney falls even further below the heroic standard; already engaged to a girl of good family, and soon learning Charity for an orphan dependent upon Lawyer Royall, Harney nevertheless grasps at the season's diversion. It is the girl, yearning for something better than the village has marked out for her, and continuing to adore the architect even after she has recognized the fleetingness of his desire; it is Charity who holds the reader's interest against men whom society has placed above her by birth, education, and material advantage.

Between the publication of *Ethan Frome* and *Summer*, Edith Wharton wrote a novel upon a theme which several times stirred her feminism to bitter depths, and that is the double standard. *The Reef* (1912) tells the story of the defiler himself undefiled. In the private and personal side of his life, George Darrow had seldom dropped below current standards, and even those declines had been brief, parenthetical, incidental. "In the recognized essentials he had always remained strictly within the limit of his scruples." His scruples did not exclude an interval at a hotel with a young girl during a time when he considered himself engaged to another woman. He was approaching forty; the girl, scarcely out of her teens. She was penniless, alone, and without sex experience; he was a successful career diplomat, and if his pursuit of the Lady Ulrica in London gave indication, had managed during his stay at various embassies to avoid a rigid celibacy. But with Darrow's past the author has little concern; she focuses upon his attitude toward the interlude spent with Sophie Viner.

In his sight, the affair has irretrievably damaged Sophie, with the result that she is unfit to act as governess to the daughter of Anna Leath, whom Darrow intends to marry. The idea of confiding the child Effie to Miss Viner he finds "peculiarly repugnant," although he does not question his own suitability for the role of stepfather, any more than he questions his right to marry the child's mother, at the termination of his former liaison. Indeed, he has all but forgotten this deviation from "his own standard of sentimental loyalty" until the girl's surprising reappearance forces him to remember her—and "mainly as the chance instrument of his lapse." Immediately he begins opposing her contemplated marriage to the stepson of his fiancée.

The critic Robert Morss Lovett finds in George Darrow an answer to the charge that Mrs. Wharton could not draw men. George Darrow, according to this appraiser, is as fully realized as Lily Bart. But does any critic claim Darrow to be the spiritual equal of Lily? It is Sophie who merits comparison with the heroine of *The House of Mirth*. Like Lily, Sophie makes a complete sacrifice of herself, not by death, but by a return to the abhorrent drudgery she has been fleeing when her umbrella touches Darrow's on the pier at Dover. In addition to Sophie, *The Reef* contains Anna Leath, one of the largest personalities Mrs. Wharton ever evoked. The marvel of Anna Leath's magnanimity is that it does not seem marvelous, a mere fiction set up for the purposes of the story. Besides either Sophie or Anna, George Darrow would appear inconsequential; their combined excellence almost obliterates him as a moral entity.

The Reef by no means exhausted Mrs. Wharton's meditation on the double standard. *Old New York*

(1924), both in *The Old Maid* and in *New Year's Day,* directs attention to the same problem. Charlotte Lovell, name character of *The Old Maid,* has borne an illegitimate child to a man who, between steamship sailings, as it were, sought to console himself for the marriage of another woman, Charlotte's cousin Delia. These cousins contend almost equally for reader sympathy. Charlotte, poor relation to people of wealth, cut off from marriage because of her child, cut off from the child because of her husbandlessness; and Delia, rich but open-handed, understanding her cousin's predicament and removing every obstacle within the sanction of her conscience: such are the women of the piece. And the man, the father? The child is unknown to him; the mother has been a chance companion of passing lust; and he himself, a hitherto unsuccessful painter, has been "married years ago to a plain determined cousin, who had hunted him down in Rome, and enclosing him in unrelenting domesticity, had obliged all New York on the grand tour to buy his pictures with a resigned grimace."

In *New Year's Day,* Mrs. Wharton describes the gentle duplicity of Elizabeth Hazeldean, who is so grateful to her husband for relieving her from an orphan's dependence that, when his health and earning power fail, she quietly takes a lover. Charles Hazeldean believes that luxuries form the mainspring of his wife's existence, and in this belief Elizabeth allows him to continue until his death. But Henry Prest she disabuses of the notion that she has become his mistress through passion for himself. The fatuity of her husband she endures because she loves him; the fatuity of the man she has exploited in order to foster that love is another matter.

Again, in *New Year's Day*, Mrs. Wharton has stated a favorite thesis: that woman, suffering an economic bondage hardly known to man, and receiving an inferior measure of social tolerance, yet manages not only to captain her own soul but to exert more than reciprocal leverage on the other sex.   The same proposition is implicit in *The Mother's Recompense* (1925). Because, eighteen years prior to the opening of the story, Kate Clephane has left her husband for another man, she suffers social ostracism, the loss of her small daughter, and the realization that "the prison of her marriage had been liberty compared with what she had exchanged it for."   Dismissing her lover, she lives in strictest propriety until at the age of thirty-nine she meets Chris Fenno, like herself a wanderer over Europe. Although at pains to reconcile his intelligence with the need for casinos and rowdy crowds, Kate continues to love Fenno long after he has disappeared.   Nor does her affection entirely flee when she next encounters him —as the fiancé of her own daughter.

Chris Fenno, wavering on the border of incest, is no Sophoclean hero; he possesses not one flaw merely, and that tragic, but a general weakness of fiber.   In youth he considers himself a painter; in middle age he impresses his friends as concerned only about writing. An uneasy job-holder, he is an easy lover; as a son, he has been, by his own admission, a nuisance first and last; and, despite momentary queasiness over the prospect of his successive relationship to mother and daughter, he will doubtless enjoy his honeymoon and a share of the Clephane fortune.

For Kate Clephane the way is more difficult.   Refusing in New York both the Clephane wealth and an advantageous offer of marriage, she returns to the dreariness of the European round.   Like Sophie Viner, of *The Reef*, Kate Clephane flees a situation which her presence might seem to condone. As in *The Reef* and in *New Year's Day*, the heroine of *The Mother's Recompense* appears first victimized by man's sex logic and finally transcendent over the very code with which he sought to fetter her.

4

The heroines of Edith Wharton do not always rely on spiritual victories to mark their prowess. In *The Custom of the Country* (1913) and in *The Buccaneers* (1938), their triumph is measured by American cash and old-world titles. Undine Spragg, with only youth and sex at her command, successfully assaults first the older aristocracy of New York City, and then crosses the Atlantic to acquire a French nobleman. Bright-haired as the Medusa, devouring not only her husbands but her father and young son, Undine outrivals even Scarlett O'Hara Hamilton Kennedy Butler. Certainly in the matter of names, the Wharton heroine scores, with the final signing of herself as Undine Spragg Moffatt Marvell de Chelles Moffatt. Scarlett's bondage over Rhett Butler eventually ceases, but Elmer Moffatt, the first husband of Undine Spragg, is eager to become her fourth.

Ralph Marvell, who believes himself the partner of Undine's first marriage, lacks neither looks nor breeding. He has gone to Harvard of course, and then to Oxford; he writes a little, paints a little, and practices law after the custom of his ancestors. But against his wife he has no defense. Herself unfaithful, she secures the divorce; an unwilling and indifferent mother, she obtains custody of the child. All that remains for Ralph Marvell is to kill himself.

The titled Frenchman, Raymond de Chelles, shares aristocratic birth and wide cultural interests with the

second American husband of Undine Spragg; nor is the
man who precedes and follows them to be disregarded,
despite his lack of education and family background.
Elmer Moffatt not only makes enough money to satisfy Undine Spragg; he learns enough about art to
satisfy himself.   As a collector he manifests an aestheticism as genuine as the love he bears his wife's son.

The sex of Undine's child, who is torn first from
his real father and then from his adored "French
father," seems no matter of accident, but part of a
design, which allots a common maleness to the van-
quished, whether they submit to woman as a force for
good or evil.   *The Custom of the Country,* tracing
the destructive power of one woman over two continents, describes what the author conceives—perhaps
unconsciously—as universal female dominance.

Yet immediately such a summary of feminism in
the works of Edith Wharton is formulated, the sum-
marizer must answer to the challenge of *Bunner Sisters*
(1916).   Here is a male with power to destroy.   If
ever a man lacked mercy at the hands of his creator,
that man is Herman Ramy.   Now, it may be objected
that the whole novelette lacks mercy; that the Bunner
sisters' "small shop, in a shabby basement, in a side-
street already doomed to decline" lay disdainfully outside the social orbit of Edith Newbold Jones Wharton.
But even though the author may begin by looking
down on her characters, as the narrative progresses
compassion becomes no matter of neighborhood, and
Edith Wharton sees the poor almost with the eyes of
Dickens.

There is another fact to be weighed in the estimate
of Herman Ramy, more significant than his poverty,
and that is his nationality.   Herman was a German,

and at the time *Bunner Sisters* was written (1916)—
perhaps for the rest of the author's life—the jingle
reminded Edith Wharton of Ypres and the Marne.

But aside from his "tendency to illustrate Grimm's
law in the interchange of his consonants," Herman
Ramy was a dope-addict, a worthless watch-repairer, a
wife-deserter, a thief. His appearance? A smile
showed yellow teeth with gaps between; his bulging
forehead and side skull peered through grayish hair.
His hands were pale and broad, with knotty joints and
square, grime-rimmed fingers. Coming as Romance
to the Misses Ann Eliza and Evalina Bunner, Ramy
brought them destitution and death.

Bunner Sisters and *The Custom of the Country*,
considered in opposition to each other, might be cited
as a mutual cancellation of sex bias on the part of the
author. Herman Ramy visits upon his wife and her
sister what Undine Spragg offers her successive husbands. But *The Custom of the Country* is fashioned
in the spirit of comedy; even the sound of Ralph
Marvell's gun at his own temple can hardly be heard
above the uproar of Undine's social conquest. Also,
the economic situation of the victim must be taken
into account. Raymond de Chelles forced to sell ancestral tapestries and Miss Ann Eliza Bunner turned out
of her shop do not put the same question to Provi-
dence. Finally, in writing these diverse tales of sexual
dupery, the author has pleaded the weakness of
woman. A man seduced will conceal his plight for
fear of laughter; a woman in the same condition—even
with benefit of clergy, as in the case of Mrs. Herman
Ramy—has deeper dread. Instead of reversing the
judgment implicit in *The Custom of the Country*, a
novel published three years earlier, *Bunner Sisters* adds

another item to Edith Wharton's long indictment of masculinity.

At the end of her life Edith Wharton found no reason to alter the conviction which charged her maturity. Although a posthumous fragment, *The Buccaneers* (1938) establishes through its ground-plan an essential likeness to *The Custom of the Country* (1913). Each novel pictures the assault of a new upon an entrenched society. Undine Spragg, representing the plutocracy, conquers the aristocracy not only in New York but abroad; Nan St. George, an obscure American girl still in her 'teens, not only marries the greatest catch in England but, wearying of ducal dullness, changes over to another titled Englishman.

Or fitting masculine and feminine elements into a different pattern from that formed by defeated and conquering social groups, the heroine's part may be assigned to Laura Testvalley, the English governess of Italian ancestry who engineers the invasion of England. If in aiding her former pupil, Nan, to quit the Duke of Tintagel for a more likely lover, Miss Testvalley loses Sir Helmsley Thwarte, and with him the hope of an easy old age, she but reinforces a position persistently held by the author; namely, that it is the woman who acts as free moral agent.

It is the woman who chooses, whether her lover be the Duke of Tintagel or the Duke of Pianura. With the exception of *Bunner Sisters,* every novel that Edith Wharton ever wrote shows the woman triumphant, either spiritually after the manner of Lily Bart or in the predatory fashion of Undine Spragg. And, to emphasize the degree of feminine achievement, Mrs. Wharton places her women characters against men of the worthiest type.

Edith Wharton's novels begin and end with a duke: a reigning prince of the Po Valley, during the eighteenth century, when the glory of the Renaissance still lingered over Italy; the first peer of England, when the sun was content to trace its orbit around British possessions. In France Mrs. Wharton found the great aristocrat, Raymond de Chelles, who would have ornamented any drawing-room known to Marcel Proust, and with more serenity and kindliness than are usually encountered in *A La Recherche du Temps Perdu*. When Edith Wharton sought out her own people, they were men like Ralph Marvell or Newland Archer, descendants of families who had enjoyed generations of cultivated leisure; or if she wandered beyond the limits of daily acquaintance to areas and strata which her artist's sympathy readily encompassed, halting in Starkfield, Massachusetts, or in the Middle West, she picked a man "head and shoulders above his fellows"—Ethan Frome or Lawyer Royall, Dexter Manford or Vance Weston.

Yet, the author's high choice notwithstanding, "there are," according to Edmund Wilson, "no first-rate men in the novels of Edith Wharton." And Robert Herrick has claimed that "Mrs. Wharton's stories are almost manless, in any real conception of the sex. . . ."

If Edith Wharton has deliberately muted masculine character in order to show it subservient to feminine, the question may well be asked, What gains for her heroines has she secured by such a method? To measure her women characters within the confines of her own novels is not enough; granted that they display sufficient force against the comparative weakness of their masculine antagonists, how do they appear beside heroines free of feminist bias? Or, slightly to shift the basis of inquiry, does an anti-masculinist approach to literature necessarily enhance feminine character?

Discussion will be postponed until a later chapter, after additional feminist material has been examined in the novels of Ellen Glasgow and Willa Cather.

III
ELLEN GLASGOW
Evangel Militant

ALTHOUGH from the beginning of her literary career until its close half a century later, Ellen Glasgow displayed an insistent and pertinacious feminism, she wrote one novel which seems to challenge her basic thesis. *Phases of an Inferior Planet* (1898) stands unique among the works of the author, for a number of reasons. First, it is a love story, and a love story alone. Never before the writing of this book or afterwards, did Miss Glasgow consider the interaction of man, woman, and fate sufficient reason for bringing pen to paper. Second, *Phases of an Inferior Planet* bears no social message. Its setting in New York City, this novel temporarily detaches the author from the problems of her native South. Finally, and most significantly for purposes of this study, *Phases of an Inferior Planet* aims no shafts at sexual injustice. The plight of woman in a man's world, which provides the substance of Miss Glasgow's remaining fiction, is hardly mentioned in the story of Anthony and Marianna. Indeed, this novel reverses the author's usual assignment of masculine and feminine roles. Here is the man, not the woman, deserted; here is the man, not the woman, building a public triumph over a private tragedy. In a book of many faults—a superfluity of characters, a superfluity of wit, an emergency ending —Anthony Algarcife, a young agnostic condemned to eucharistic vestments, reveals the finest personality Ellen Glasgow ever created.

Ranking very near Father Algarcife is the lawyer-politician, Nick Burr, in *The Voice of the People* (1900). Unlike *Phases of an Inferior Planet,* however, this novel carries a weight of feminine protest. Marthy Burr, Nick's aunt and stepmother, declares that if she had never toted anything heavier than a water-bucket, her back would be as straight as her husband's. Black Aunt Verbeny observes, with an irony which the author leaves the reader to surmise, that a woman no man has claimed "ain' wuth claimin'." Gently-bred Eugenia Battle gives her suitor to understand that women's skirts are the best prisons man ever invented. Feminine grievance finds expression not only upon the lips of women characters, but indirectly, through the author's exhibits of masculine fatuousness. There is Mr. Burwell, for instance, who considers his own sex capable of settling all social barriers; and the judge, who is never so discourteous as to withhold praise from a chaste woman and never so indiscreet as to admire one "wanting in the supremest of feminine virtues." But, despite the chorus of feminist disaffection, Nick Burr maintains a worthy and central position in *The Voice of the People.*

Such centrality Miss Glasgow continues to allot masculine character in her earlier novels. Again and again she rallies her plots around a hero. Not until the fiction of her artistic maturity does she focus upon a heroine. Whether such a narrative pattern was due to a beginner's respect for tradition, or whether Miss Glasgow at the outset failed to recognize the intensity of her anti-masculinist convictions, can hardly be determined. But this much appears from a study of her first works (always excepting *Phases of an Inferior*

Planet and *The Voice of the People*): that although
nominally dedicated to an exploration of masculine
character, they owe whatever significance they possess
to their substratum of feminism.   If *The Deliverance*
(1905) contains an effective personality, it is not
Christopher Blake, the dispossessed young aristocrat
whose outward actions furnish the machinery of the
plot, but his blind mother, who, although confessing
to a long and happy marriage, was glad that her
husband had never faced a choice between herself and
his dinner.   Purporting to depict the rise of an indigent
city boy, *The Romance of a Plain Man* (1909) owes
its chief interest to the women of the piece: to Mrs.
Chitling, who, during the days of agitation for equal
suffrage, declared that any honest female already in
possession of innumerable boons, such as long suffering and child-bearing, would prefer not the vote but
the respect of men; to Sally Mickleborough Starr, who
recalled that whenever Grandmamma wanted to know
whether her tooth ached, she asked Grandpapa; to
Miss Mataoca, who remained an old maid rather than
marry a man with a past.   *The Miller of Old Church*
(1911) is remembered not for the name character,
but for the man-hating Molly Merryweather, whose
mother had never had a husband; and for feminist
observations scattered throughout the book: "It's all
sensible enough to lambaste the women when they
don't pick up every virtue we throw away . . . ."
or, "It takes two to make an impropriety."

Again, in *The Builders* (1919) Miss Glasgow
attempts a masculine character of some proportion. But
David Blackburn, in spite of financial attainment,
political idealism, and devotion to wife and child, remains a robot, whose speech unrolls like so many feet
of ticker-tape.   It is the cry of Caroline Meade which

proclaims a living voice: "There must be something that one can live on beside love!" Like future heroines of Miss Glasgow's creation, the leading woman is seeking a defense against which Bluebeard himself shall not prevail. And concurrent with this *motif*— the flight from love—is the strain of sex-pity which runs throughout the works of Ellen Glasgow, a constant reiteration of the-woman-pays theme.

Similarly, the heroine of *One Man In His Time* (1922) finds reason to deprecate feminine status in a masculine world. Man assumes (falsely) that woman's part in love is as heroically passive as her role in religion; man uses woman for a peg upon which to hang his sentiments. But, even though the heroine finds masculine mental processes as dully predictable as the workings of a watch, *One Man In His Time* conforms to the early Glasgowian pattern, of shaping the narrative around masculine action. Gideon Vetch, circus-born governor of Virginia, brings to a halt, however, the procession of vigorous and youthful males which the author purports to honor with the hero's mantle.

2

If the hero's mantle hangs slackly upon robust shoulders, Miss Glasgow fails to convince the reader of its becomingness to men broken by adversity. In *The Wheel of Life* (1906) Roger Adams, ill and burdened by debt, devotes himself through her last illness to a luxury-mad, concupiscent wife. But within the same book, two libertines crowd the alleged hero almost off the page; and what margin they leave is monopolized by a feminist heroine, who has observed that men are not born monogamous, that they mistake convention for virtue, and control women not only by their laws but by their jokes.

Daniel Ordway of *The Ancient Law* (1908) who has been sent to prison through the extravagance of his wife, bears credentials of sanctity as authentic as Roger Adams, but, withal, remains a deadly piece of characterization, fulfilling the hero's role in the dullest of Ellen Glasgow's books. Lacking even the feminism which usually sparkles from her stories, *The Ancient Law* is interesting only because it marks the author's final attempt to deal with a saint. Unless Anthony Algarcife count as an exception (and the young priest considered himself a seeker after knowledge rather than virtue), the dominantly spiritual personality seems to elude Miss Glasgow, as the man of extraordinary physical drive (again with a possible exception in Nick Burr) remains beyond her grasp.

But the literary purpose of Ellen Glasgow was not to be accomplished through the glorification of masculine character. Her mission was to magnify woman. The stories given over to a lusty male or to a broken saint are divagations from her main task, which she began with her first novel, *The Descendant* (1897).

3

In *A Certain Measure*, the final critique of her own work, Ellen Glasgow refers again and again to her first novel, often apologetically. With regard to form *The Descendant* would furnish no artist an occasion for boasting. The story begins as Michael Akersham's and ends as Rachel Gavin's, the theme begins as a defense of the individual against society and ends as a vindication of woman's rights. But despite its formal indecision, this first novel contains the germ of all that was to be significant in the future work of Ellen Glasgow.

Scarcely a feminist grievance but finds splenetic
utterance. Like Edith Wharton, Ellen Glasgow plays
with bitter stops upon the theme of the defiler undefiled. A woman who, as in the case of Rachel
Gavin, surrenders virginity without marriage suffers
irretrievable damage, whereas the masculine participant
escapes unblemished. Nor is the author content to
ridicule male sex-logic in the present tense; the whole
tradition of feminine chastity as against masculine
promiscuity receives an airing in the recollected actions
of the heroine's greatgrandfather and greatgrand-
mother. But, the author delights in pointing out,
man's essential instability reveals itself no more
through sexual behavior than through his general
unwillingness to endure the pain of any ideal. An
illegitimate poverty-driven child, Michael Akersham
challenged convention only so long as he remained
personally unacceptable; but Rachel Gavin waged war
in the name of righteousness throughout her life. Finally, Miss Glasgow shows the sexes as each realizing
a proper reward: the hero paying with death for his
moral vacillation, the heroine surviving her love in
desirelessness. Through *The Descendant,* a work of
confused purpose, with a title which might apply
equally to Akersham, offspring of an unlicensed mat-
ing, or to Rachel Gavin, rebellious heir to the canon
of feminine submissiveness, Ellen Glasgow found the
formula which was to serve her, often with distinction,
over a period of fifty years.

4

Between publication of *The Descendant* and of the
half-dozen novels on which her reputation rests, Ellen
Glasgow wrote three others which served increasingly
to clarify her theme. *The Battle-Ground* (1902)
voices it but dimly; *Life and Gabriella* (1916) states

it so harshly as to alienate reader sympathy; *Virginia* (1920) makes of feminism almost a song.

The Battle-Ground, a study of the sexes as the South conditioned them during and immediately prior to the Civil War, acidly distinguishes between the lot of the planter and the lot of the planter's wife. The master stands between Doric columns, looking complacently upon the fat lands of his inheritance, while the mistress busies herself with slaves, storerooms, sewing, children. And, Miss Glasgow implies, except for the war, this sexual division of idleness and labor might have continued, with "Beau" Montjoy, after a roysterer's life at college, coming into the prerogatives of a well-fed country gentleman, and Betty Ambler following the industrious example of her mother.

And yet, although lauding woman not only for her superior practicality and wisdom, and deprecating the military as one more proof of masculine vanity and sex-despotism, *The Battle-Ground* carries a mild and even kindly expression of feminist doctrine. If Mrs. Ambler tells her daughter that women do not need as much sense as men, Mr. Ambler tells his wife that only her sex prevented her from being President. If "Beau" Montjoy makes a parade of temper, prodigality, and cocksureness, he lives to retrace his steps in broken humility. Except for a single paragraph, *The Battle-Ground* might be dismissed as a conventional, if slightly tart, story of the Civil War. This paragraph frames the musings of Betty Ambler on an early glimpse of her sweetheart. Young Montjoy has gone whistling into a burning Negro cabin, to bring out a baby in his coat; re-emerging he has coolly taken up the broken air.

Three decades after *The Battle-Ground,* Ellen Glasgow wrote a novel called *The Sheltered Life*

(1934), in which Eva Birdsong reflects on an early glimpse of her husband. George Birdsong has stopped playing ball long enough to rescue a baby from a burning Negro shanty; re-emerging he has coolly taken back his ball. The rescued Negro child, Memoria, grew up to become not only washerwoman to Eva and George Birdsong after their highly romantic marriage, but mistress to George as well.

Comparing the deed of black Memoria's white lover with the almost duplicate act of bravery which roused Betty Ambler to romantic reverie, the reader wonders what seed of disdain was present at the conception of Dan Montjoy, hero of *The Battle-Ground*.

Fourteen years elapsed between the writing of *The Battle-Ground* and *Life with Gabriella*. Meanwhile the author had been fumbling with the novel as a vehicle for an important male character. *Phases of an Inferior Planet* and *The Voice of the People* lay behind her; and since publication of *The Battle-Ground* she had been turning out fiction in a manner of routine. Nor did she distinguish herself through *Life and Gabriella*. Here is the feminine protest without benefit of humor. Husbands swagger under several names, but with a common perfidy, drunken, lecherous, and financially incompetent. So explicit are her charges against the other sex that Miss Glasgow feels called on to deny (through the reflections of her heroine) any intended malice. "Against men as men she had never even thought of cherishing a grievance." But the deserted wife appears too often and too pathetically for the author to salvage much of a case for men. Tucked in at the end of the novel, to be sure, is the self-made Irishman, Ben O'Hara, who has worked his way up from the cellar—literally, for such was the

place of his birth.   But the reader recognizes Ben as
a concession to the happy ending.   *Life and Gabriella*
celebrates not the triumph of Eros but the triumph of
Athena, in the guise of couturière.   Subtitled "The
Story of a Woman's Courage," *Life and Gabriella*
looks ahead to a greater heroine, who even more convincingly was to prove how little woman needs man
in her march toward victory—Dorinda Oakley of
Barren Ground.

Between positive assertions of feminism, Ellen
Glasgow was to demonstrate the obverse aspect of her
thesis. *Virginia* (1920) tells the story of a woman in
defeat.   Although through author's asides Miss
Glasgow explains that not only time but the bustling
times conspired against this gently reared daughter of
the Old South, the reader is persuaded of the husband's complicity.   Oliver Treadwell represents Miss
Glasgow's apotheosis of compromise, and the more
shoddy in the unflickering light of his wife's devotion.
Yet by mob standards, Oliver would make a good
showing.   Recently returned from the altitudes of
European culture, he was willing in the lowlands of
the *post-bellum* South to half-starve for truth.   As a
young husband he held out the length of many argu-
ments before permitting Virginia to make the morning
fires and prepare hot yeast rolls for breakfast. Smart-
ing under the failure of a play which had actually
climbed to the boards, he tried to mask the irritation
that small romping children may cause a bookish
father.   Even after his wife began to bore him, he
contented himself with platonic affairs until a new
marriage became professionally desirable.   Finally, in
the matter of his art, if the public refused to see the
plays he wished to write, should he have refused them

the plays they wished to see?   Virginia, Miss Glasgow declares, lost everything; but Miss Glasgow does not forget to ask the reader what Oliver Treadwell had ever had.

5

Virginia, according to the author's estimate in *A Certain Measure,* was an expressive novel, but inferior to *Barren Ground,* through which Miss Glasgow felt herself to be fully articulate for the first time.   She saw, as the novel unfolded, a complete reversal of a classic situation.   "For once, in Southern fiction, the betrayed woman would become the victor instead of the victim."   In making this comment, Miss Glasgow apparently forgot her own previous reversal of the situation in *The Descendant,* published two decades before *Barren Ground;* and, attempting to establish the uniqueness of Dorinda Oakley, ignored the heroine of *Life and Gabriella.*   If the thought of love, the faintest reminder of its potency, filled Dorinda Oakley with aversion, the very memory of the emotion which drew men and women together filled Gabriella with repulsion.   If Dorinda, after she had been betrayed by a lover, reflected exultantly on Old Farm, Gabriella, after she had been betrayed by a husband, reflected with similar enthusiasm on Mme Dinard's dressmaking establishment.   Any reader who recalls Gabriella's proud claim to hardness " . . . if I'd been soft, I should have broken long ago," will be prepared for Dorinda's boast of being through with soft things.

The foundation pattern of *Barren Ground* is not new, certainly not in the hands of this particular author.   But now, with the story of Dorinda Oakley, Miss Glasgow adds an element which will prove useful in such succeeding works as *The Sheltered Life*

(1934), *Vein of Iron* (1935), and *In This Our Life* (1941).   To complete her derogation of sex, she introduces a man whom the years have rendered meek; Pa Oakley, in *Barren Ground,* who was so different from the usual male that his own wife felt impelled to praise him at the expense of their son.

Whether Pa Oakley was good only in old age—or, as his wife implied, always—there is little doubt that Dorinda Oakley's lover, Jason Greylock, was consistently evil.   Perhaps less evil than irresolute, unable to carry out his own intention, whether it were to continue practicing medicine in the North or to marry the girl he had got with child.   And while Jason Greylock sinks beneath his own weakness, Dorinda Oakley rises by her strength.

Dying as ignominiously as Michael Akersham of *The Descendant* or George Fowler of *Life and Gabriella,* Jason Greylock suffers a more detailed ruin than the earlier heroes.   The author of *Barren Ground* has come into her own, not only with a theme, but with its ripe expression.   No longer does she allow the reader to surmise dimly the stages by which a betrayer reaches his doom; *Barren Ground* paints step by step the hero's loss of community respect, domestic harmony, personal health.   His medical practice gone, his wife a suicide, his body wasted by alcohol, Jason is obliged to surrender his farm to the woman whom he has earlier failed.

Even Dorinda wondered why she wanted that piece of land.   She already controlled her own and the good acres of her husband.   "Was it merely that the possession of Five Oaks would complete her victory and his degradation?"

Her victory and his degradation: such is the theme not only of *Barren Ground* but of all the author's succeeding novels. Although two light pieces, *The Romantic Comedians* (1926) and *They Stooped to Folly* (1929), interpose themselves chronologically, the mood of *Barren Ground* will be continued by discussion of *The Sheltered Life*.

The Sheltered Life (1934) brings to a head Ellen Glasgow's long musing on the sexual division of labor; rather, the division into labor for one sex, idleness for the other. Over a period of many years and through many novels Miss Glasgow shows the manner in which the male insulates his sloth in the sheathings of a profession, while the woman carries the burden of existence. And this disparity is fixed, regardless of the class described. There are exceptions, of course, parasitic wives like Connie Adams or Angela Blackburn in the minor novels, or Janet Rowan and the younger Timberlake girl in the novels of the author's maturity. But these are the chaff which Ellen Glasgow deliberately scatters, that the women of fiber may stand, and the more clearly in the very books where a female wastrel has been exploiting her sex. Yet even taking into account all the masculine drudges, from Roger Adams (1906) to Asa Timberlake (1941), there are few men in the novels of Ellen Glasgow who labor creatively. Even Adams and Timberlake, the most industrious of Miss Glasgow's masculine characters, are driven from without. It is the women who travail with selfless joy, and not in childbirth alone.

The difference is this, as Ellen Glasgow sees it: man, the red-blooded male of woman's fancy, relishes but two activities, sexual intercourse and the kill; whereas the whole of life is woman's concern. The characters of George and Eva Birdsong (*The Sheltered Life*) make bitterly clear what Miss Glasgow had been struggling to say. In her first book, *The*

Descendant, she had shown the heroine's ancestress spinning at the hearth, while the ancestor roistered at the tavern. As far back as *The Battle-Ground,* she had pictured the man as essentially a drone, calling himself a planter but shoving off on his wife a burden heavier than his slaves could have been compelled to bear. "Of all the souls on the great plantation, the mistress alone had never rested from her labors." In *The Voice of the People,* not only a gentleman like Mr. Battle sat while his sister bustled from kitchen to smokehouse to poultry-yard; the elder Burr, an unsuccessful peanut farmer, clung to a chair just as tenaciously. *The Ancient Law* described the aristocratic Beverly Brooke, whose wife had borne nine children, and whose family would have been on the county except for the efforts of a half-sister; sighed Mr. Brooke: "If things had only come out as I planned them . . . my wife would never have raised her finger except to lift food to her lips." But a person who had lived in the Brooke household remarked: "I've seen him send her downstairs a dozen times a day to make him a lemonade." The contrast in *Virginia* between the woman's exertion as wife and mother and the man's as soured intellectual and commercial playwright has already been mentioned. *Barren Ground* no longer designates the homeplace after Dorinda has taken charge: "If I couldn't do better than the men about here, I'd be a mighty poor farmer!"

Even *Vein of Iron* fails to convince the reader that the cerebral busyness of John Fincastle amounts to as much as Grandmother Fincastle's knitting and washing and cooking, her care of the sick and assistance at childbirth; and as for Ralph McBride, compared with his wife, he seems only another idler on Ellen Glasgow's list.

But it is George Birdsong who wastes time with the sunniest conscience. He is a lawyer; that is, he keeps hours at a law office. Let his wife absent herself on a brief and rare vacation, and his home lapses into wilderness.

One occupation, however, he follows with zest, and that is duck-hunting. Never does Miss Glasgow describe a character with more acid zest than George Birdsong in the act of picking up and laying down dead birds. But no sooner have hunting and the spoils of death temporarily released their hold upon his "open mind and heart" than George resumes his other interest—woman, that is; and so open are his mind and heart that he discriminates against neither color nor age.

George's wife, unlike Gabriella Fowler, has no dressmaking establishment to fall back on; unlike Dorinda Oakley, she has no farm. Ada McBride, in *Vein of Iron*, can return to a department store, and Roy Timberlake, doubly-deceived heroine of *In This Our Life*, has her decorating shop. But Eva Birdsong has only George—the boy who ran into a burning shanty to rescue a pickaninny.

Through this single act of short-pants heroism, he has secured an illusion which lasts his wife until the moment when, suddenly blinking past the earlier image, she perceives him for what he is, as the reader has long since perceived him: a man leisurely resuming his coat in the house of a Negro mistress; a man who fancies himself too much to have his shirts ironed at a common laundry; a man fond of his stomach; a man who kills time with almost the same zest that he kills birds. And to him Eva Birdsong, childless and jobless, must look for salvation.

Yet not to him alone. There remains General
Archbald, appointed by the author to prove that all
men are not hunters of animals and women. Grandfather of Jennie Blair Archbald, whose youthful amor-
ousness precipitates the murder of George Birdsong,
the General is described as a rebel even in youth against
the predatory instincts of his sex. Reflective, gentle,
humane, General Archbald looks back, through his
intrinsic virtue, to Pa Oakley of *Barren Ground,* and
through his cultivated understanding to John Fincastle
in *Vein of Iron.*

An unfrocked Presbyterian minister, whose denial
of the Virgin Birth and publication of a many-
volumed work, *God as Idea,* have set him on the road
to starvation, John Fincastle helps to fix the basic
pattern of Ellen Glasgow's last novels. The design is
quadrilateral, with one character, who may be described
as masculine-neuter, sustaining the counter-claims of
the lover, and the other two sides being occupied by
women, one intelligent, courageous, and consistently
ill-served, the other flighty and brainless, yet able to
gain her way.

By this unjust ordering of fate, the superior
woman is, according to her temperament, furiously
affronted (as in the case of Dorinda Oakley or Roy
Timberlake) or (after the fashion of Eva Birdsong
and Ada Fincastle) wretchedly grieved. But whatever
the reaction of his put-upon wife or mistress, the man
remains substantially the same in four novels and
under five different names.

Ralph McBride in *Vein of Iron* follows a path
already grooved by Jason Greylock of *Barren Ground.*
Ralph marries Janet Rowan because "they" brought
pressure, as Jason married Geneva Ellgood for the

same reason.   As Jason botched a medical career,
Ralph botches a legal career.   As Jason left Dorinda
Oakley to bear an illegitimate child, so Ralph McBride
leaves Ada Fincastle.   And although divorce from his
wife and marriage with the mother of his child par-
tially rehabilitates young McBride, no outward force
can preserve him from the working of inner weakness.
A second time he brings misfortune to the Fincastle
family, this time hastening the death of his second
wife's father.

Ellen Glasgow's final novel, *In This Our Life,*
again utilizes the quadrilateral found in *Barren
Ground, The Sheltered Life,* and *Vein of Iron.*   Asa
Timberlake, with a record of having done everything
he was obliged to do and nothing that he would have
liked to do, immediately recalls David Archbald, who
had nothing that he wanted but everything that was
good for him.   The author's summaries of the two
men are not identical; nor is Archbald as young as
the fifty-nine-year-old Timberlake; but the men have
years enough in common and a shared predisposition
toward quiet endurance sufficient to make one an easy
substitute for the other in the now-familiar formula
whereby Ellen Glasgow groups the masculine-neuter,
the villain-lover, and two women.

The virtuous Timberlake is opposed by a pair of
villain-lovers.   For general untrustworthiness, Craig
Fleming and Peter Kingmill can hardly be told apart.
Each is the dupe of the same oversexed woman; one
botches a legal career; the other, a career in medicine.
Peter Kingmill, sometimes husband to both Timberlake sisters, has red hair and brown eyes like an earlier
doctor of Miss Glasgow's creation, Jason Greylock;
and also like the hero of *Barren Ground,* this medical

man keeps a whiskey bottle handy. And the lawyer, floundering in his profession, floundering in and out of love, recalls the unstable hero in *Vein of Iron.*

On the feminine side of the quadrilateral are the two daughters of Asa Timberlake, christened respectively Roy and Stanley. The industry and rectitude of the elder sister, Roy Timberlake Kingmill, earn her desertion in turn by husband and fiancé; while Stanley Timberlake Kingmill, an adulteress, a motivating cause of her husband's suicide, and a hit-and-run driver, continues an uninterrupted march over masculine hearts, including even those of the policeman detailed to investigate the murder of a child.

Such is the pattern Miss Glasgow traces in the last of her serious novels. Although her comedies employ a different basic scheme, they in no wise disturb the ranking of the sexes as previously established.

6

In setting out to exploit the meanness of humanity, classical comedy used the term *man* generically, playing beams of malice alike upon male and female. But the comedies of Ellen Glasgow are ordered to illuminate the foibles of men. In *The Romantic Comedians* (1926), which a contemporary critic has designated as not only the perfect novel of its kind but the one novel in English worthy of such praise, the author constantly derides her masculine characters, denying them even the virtues of old age. Conversationally, of course, the women of the piece score always, through barbs aimed at masculine obtuseness, fatuity, and lasciviousness. But situation, even more effectively than epigram, contributes to feminine victory. Sexagenarian Judge Honeywell, abandoned by his young wife for a man of her own age, is well enough

served for ignoring a spinster who had waited from
her youth; while Annabel Honeywell, the decamping
wife, displays only feminine shrewdness in holding on
to the judge long enough to provide for her mother
and vary her own regimen of fried liver and cast-off
clothing.

For her second essay in mirth, *They Stooped to
Folly* (1929), Ellen Glasgow chooses the fallen
woman as a theme.   Three generations of strayed
chastity are exhibited: Aunt Agatha, whom the pressure of tradition had turned from a spirited girl into
an elderly Magdalen; Mrs. Dalrymple, who, unde-
feated by the simultaneous loss of reputation, husband,
and lover, had made a second marriage, richer than her
first, and had acquired a reputation for war work;
and Milly Burden, an unmarried stenographer, who,
despite the birth of a stillborn child, refused to consider herself a ruined woman.

And the men who severally precipitated the fall of
these ladies?   Aunt Agatha never gave her partner a
name, since, according to ancient ritual, the true
woman in dishonor preserved her guilty secret to the
grave; and Miss Agatha was a true woman.   Mrs.
Dalrymple never needed to name her lover; everybody
in town was presumed to know him.   What the
reader fails to find out about the other men must be
supplied hypothetically by the lover of Milly Burden.
To stand up for his sex against three generations of
wronged women requires a firmer character than
Martin Welding; literary and shell-shocked, the young
veteran lacks sufficiency even for one generation.

Although Welding does not sustain the masculine
role unassisted, he receives slight help from the brothers Littlepage, Virginius and the vagabond artist
Marmaduke.   The eccentric one-legged painter has

only the philosopher's part in the action; and Virginius, father-in-law to Welding and employer of the young man's former mistress, cannot resist carrying on a flirtation with Mrs. Dalrymple while his own wife is dying of cancer.

7

In her comedies as in her serious novels, Ellen Glasgow significantly advances but a single thesis, that man is the enemy of woman. The comedies rout him with ridicule and edged contempt; the serious novels display his dead body as proof of love's futility. *The Descendant*, written by a girl of eighteen, describes the heroine gloating over her lover's drawn face and whole ruined length, "the broken and wasted remains of a great vitality." Published fifty years later, *In This Our Life* dwells on the corpse of another lover, Peter Kingmill, whose "dynamic sensuality had become simply a boxful of refuse to be carted away." Such a meditation on demolished virility appears not only in the beginning and final works by Ellen Glasgow; it occurs throughout her novels. The heroine of *Life and Gabriella* has the double satisfaction of beholding her husband in death and of recognizing in the manner of his demise a reversal of anti-feminist tradition; here the betrayed has triumphed, not the betrayer. Perhaps the most famous character created by the author, Dorinda Oakley, of *Barren Ground*, enjoyed the knowledge that before actually tumbling into his drunkard's grave, Jason Greylock had kept alive on whiskey and persimmons. The heroine of *The Sheltered Life*, however, did not wait on tuberculosis or *delirium tremens* to deliver over an erring partner; what Rachel Gavin and Dorinda Oakley relied on circumstances to effect, Eva Birdsong accomplished with her own revolver.

Opposing the villainy of her young heroes, Ellen Glasgow presents a group of aging contemplative men, such as General Archbald of *The Sheltered Life* and Dr. John Fincastle in *Vein of Iron*. Not that all the old men drawn by Miss Glasgow are admirable. A young roysterer could hardly receive more disdain from his creator than the senescent William Fitzroy of *In This Our Life*, or Judge Gamaliel Bland Honeywell, who despite his sixty-five years clung to the role of romantic comedian. Miss Glasgow writes with kindliness only of those old men for whom—to use William James' famous phrase—"the uproar of sex is over."

Such, for the purpose of this study, is the notable fact to be gleaned from the fiction of Ellen Glasgow: that sexuality and virtue are incompatible within the frame of masculine character. In no major work from the publication of *Virginia*, which may be reckoned as the author's first demonstration of mature powers, does a man of questing virility appear but to dupe or otherwise humiliate a woman spiritually his superior. Oliver Treadwell, Jason Greylock, Ralph McBride, George Birdsong, Peter Kingmill, Craig Fleming—each desolates the woman for whom he has symbolized fulfillment. Nor is one villainous hero to be confused with the other; such are the author's gifts that each betrayer remains sharply individualized. By multiplying particularized instances, Miss Glasgow seeks to establish the general truth of her proposition, that men, until winnowed by the years, bring only rue in their wake. Rue, that is, to women; for Ellen Glasgow presents masculine character primarily as it subserves feminine.

IV

WILLA CATHER

THE FEMINISM of Willa Cather is more subtle
than that of Edith Wharton or Ellen Glasgow. Mrs.
Wharton takes a stand far above her masculine characters, reluctantly admitting the necessity of their
presence at her assemblies. Miss Glasgow never denies her rapier; there are times when she admits to a
bludgeon; and always she is forthright in her use of
the novel as a means of avenging her sex. But Miss
Cather professes a different literary mission; she comes
to her heroes as friend. And it is true that within her
stories male characterization seems colored neither by
hauteur nor spleen. Miss Cather envisages masculinity
through the eyes of a kindly tutor or a warm-hearted
elder sister—except in the case of her first novel.

Unlike the books on which the author's fame rests,
Alexander's Bridge (1912) assigns the principal role
to a man. Nor is he stamped from the pattern usually
associated with a Cather hero: the basically decent
youth, conspicuous for his clean behavior, chivalry,
and good sportsmanship.

Bartley Alexander is neither young nor notably
decent. The episodes which comprise *Alexander's
Bridge* find the name character already in his forties,
and reveal him not only as adulterer but, in a sense, as
murderer and suicide. Yet Alexander is a hero accord-

ing to classic definition; that is, a man of good will marred by a tragic flaw.

In middle age and the most spectacular bridge engineer of his generation, he carries the same curse—and the same blessing—as he had during college days: an unwillingness to accept limitation. He wants his wife and professional attainment, even at the price of drudgery and the encaging duties of the civic man; he wants his mistress and the vagabondage of an unknown dreamer. He knows that he cannot have both, just as he knows that he must choose between building a cheap safe bridge and, at the same unit price, the longest cantilever in the world. But he cannot choose; that is his tragedy, the tragedy of all men who in full awareness of mortality continue to act like gods.

Such masculine behavior Willa Cather was soon to repudiate. Significantly enough, the chief figure in her second novel is called Alexandra. And henceforward there is to be no shuttling back and forth in distributing roles of strength; these are uniformly preëmpted by women characters, unless weakness be the portion of both sexes. Such is the case of *One of Ours* (1922), published during the same year as the second edition of *Alexander's Bridge*. For the reprint the author wrote a preface, in which she explained that this first novel dealt with material that was not her own.

What Miss Cather means by "an author's own material" is conjectural. She may have implied that *Alexander's Bridge*, with scenes laid in Boston and London, involves subject matter foreign to an author whose true habitat is rural Nebraska or small-town Colorado; or she may have been claiming by right of sympathy a closer affiliation with more recent immigrants than with the descendants of the original English settlers; or she may have been disclaiming the philosophy of her first novel as inconsistent with the views of a writer laboring toward the quietism of *Death Comes for the Archbishop* (1927).

However Miss Cather may have defined literary material, she was well advised in staking off certain portions as her own. A valid title for her might be bounded by *O Pioneers!* (1913), *The Song of the Lark* (1915), and *My Ántonia* (1918). Sharper contrast with her first work, the story of a man in disintegration and defeat, could hardly be presented than these three succeeding novels, which sing of triumph and a woman. What happened to his bridge is in essence what happened to Bartley Alexander: the span went into the river, "literally tearing itself to pieces, because no integral part could bear for an instant the enormous strain loosed upon it." But Willa Cather's trio of heroic women can bear any amount of strain. Firmly coördinated, stress-sustaining in every member, the personality of Alexandra Bergson, of Thea Kronborg, of Ántonia Shimerda remains a unit, regardless of live load or dead.

2

The men of these books are neither literary accessories, after the fashion of Edith Wharton's masculine characters, nor enemies to be hunted down with the weapons of Ellen Glasgow; they are likeable young men, and well individualized. Matched in mediocrity with women characters, they might show some force; but against the vigor of Miss Cather's feminine protagonists, these pleasant mannered, smooth-faced youths appear emasculate.

The first of the many acceptable young men created by Willa Cather is Emil Bergson of *O Pioneers!*

Tall, broad-shouldered, and obliging, he fits amiably into the matrix designed by the author for future heroes, who will, like himself, move in the giant shadow cast by a woman. Emil has no real part in taming the wild Nebraska tableland; even his elder brothers, Lou and Oscar, stronger men, though less agreeable, than himself, labor under the direction of Alexandra Bergson, to whose guidance their father at death has pledged them.

The Swedish pioneer, John Bergson, recognizes the superior will and endurance of his daughter, as he perhaps recognizes the superiority of his wife. Alternately accumulating and paying off debt, Bergson has little to show for a dozen years of toil. But his wife, by forcing her men to build a log house instead of contenting themselves with a sod house, by refusing to discard European custom even in a primitive environment, has preserved her family from moral laxness. The tenacity of Mrs. Bergson is more than equalled by her daughter, under whose hands the Bergson farm becomes a show-place of the region. "Any one thereabouts would have told you that was one of the richest farms on the Divide, and that the farmer was a woman . . ."

Next in vividness to Alexandra is the portrait of Emil Bergson's mistress. As Marie Tovesky, sitting on the shoulder of her Uncle Joe, drew attention from every customer in the general store where the action of *O Pioneers!* begins, so Marie Shabata, young wife of the spoiled, too-handsome immigrant, Frank Shabata, makes every appearance a stellar vehicle. Even in death her lover becomes a mere adjunct to a tragedy which is primarily hers.

The presence either of sister or of mistress would have doomed Emil Bergson to a minor role; depreciated by their combined forcefulness, he fails to achieve so much as a separate personality. Now he makes himself known to the reader as the baby brother of Alexandra Bergson, now as the junior lover of Marie Shabata; to status in his own right Emil Bergson never quite lays claim.

The remaining characters of *O Pioneers!* render a similarily negative account of their sex. As John Bergson lays a more feeble hand upon a new environment than does his wife, so Oscar and Lou Bergson, although grudging the leadership of their sister, owe to Alexandra a prosperity beyond their own mean vision. And Alexandra's late-chosen fiancé, Carl Linstrum, seems a poor consort for a woman five years his senior and a master-farmer. While still a boy Linstrum has been glad enough to quit the farm adjoining the Bergsons; nor has he found anchorage in any other occupation, whether as an engraver in Chicago or a prospector in the Klondike. Yet his attraction for Alexandra appears plausible enough; he is an evocation — somewhat frayed, to be sure — of her dead brother Emil.

Through the relationship of Linstrum and Alexandra may be traced the emotional pattern not only of *O Pioneers!* but of every significant novel by Willa Cather. It is not a sexual pattern; it is the attitude of an older sister compassionately viewing all men as juniors.

Such an attitude is repeated in *The Song of the Lark* (1915), another story of feminine achievement against, in part at least, a pioneer environment. Out of a meager childhood and scant educational opportunity, Thea Kronborg wins stardom at the Metropolitan Opera House and international recognition for her Wagnerian interpretations. Yet the world of art by no means limits her laurels; she is given romance also, with a choice of three admirers.

The first is Dr. Howard Archie, of Thea's hometown. Only his wife fails to appreciate the excellence of Dr. Archie. The Kronborgs value him as physician and friend, Thea especially. He rescues her from pneumonia, he lends her money for study abroad. The doctor's wife has reason to acknowledge indebtedness, also—her sisters are grateful enough for Belle Archie's marriage; but Belle herself, brainless and stingy, grows almost equally panicked at the idea of letting dust into her house and the idea of bearing children.

Howard Archie's sufferance of such a woman would appear more impressive if offered in *The Song of the Lark* as a unique example. But Fred Ottenburg, heir to brewery millions, shows himself as abject a marriage victim as the doctor. Like Archie, Ottenburg has chivalrously delivered himself over to an unworthy woman; and his fortuitous release, in time to become Thea's husband, adds little to his character.

Third, there is Ray Kennedy, the freight-conductor whose life insurance policy provides the send-off for a Wagnerian soprano. Kennedy exists for the same reason that the Mexican laborer from Thea's hometown comes to a performance at the Metropolitan Opera House; he exists as a bearer of homage to a heroine named Thea. *The Song of the Lark* contains as humble a cast of tributary males as can be found even in a feminist novel.

My Ántonia (1918), the final member of the trilogy dedicated to heroic women, is not so much a novel as a collection of loose sketches, scarcely held together by the name character. And those parts concerned with the heroine relate her story most circuitously. For the unfolding of so slight a tale, the use of several narrators seems hard to justify, especially in the matter of Jim Burden. He contributes nothing to the action, and his point-of-view as spectator could be spared. But he is another put-upon husband; and even though his domestic difficulties are irrelevant to Ántonia's story, they fit into the author's larger message, implied by her work as a whole. Throughout Willa Cather's novels, no circumstance is so variously detailed as the plight of a superior man in the marriage trap.

As previously noted, *The Song of the Lark* makes a double bid for reader sympathy through the similar situations of Howard Archie and Frederick Ottenburg. Other novels of Willa Cather describe the helplessness of Claude Wheeler before the prim vegetarian Enid; the long tribulation of Oswald Henshawe because of the vixenish Myra; the cross laid upon Professor St. Peter by his shallow materialistic wife; the weight of evil under which Henry Colbert struggled as the result of Sapphira's machinations. Thus, the presence of the narrator, Jim Burden, is seen as contributing an element almost indispensable to a novel by Willa Cather.

Alloted briefer description than Jim Burden, but more directly involved in the life of Ántonia are Larry Donovan, the passenger conductor who seduces the young Bohemian girl, and her fellow-immigrant, Cuzak, who eventually becomes her husband—"a crumpled little man, with run-over boot heels . . ." Jim Burden, Larry Donovan, and the Bohemian Cuzak earn little more distinction than the trio who helped Thea Kronborg climb from the backroom of a Moonstone, Colorado, parsonage to the center of the

Metropolitan stage. If the author's thesis were that of the Bible, *"Thine* is the glory," the absence of haloes on either sex would require no comment. But haloes are absent only from masculine brows. Never do the slick pages of a woman's magazine place a heroine more conspicuously on parade than Willa Cather places Ántonia Shimerda.

3

One of Ours (1922), the novel which follows Willa Cather's trilogy of heroic women, assigns the principal part to a man. After portraying Alexandra Bergson, who tamed wild land and prayed for the soul of her brother's murderer; after Thea Kronborg, who sang her way from poverty and drabness to the imaginative soarings of the Wagnerian repertoire; after Ántonia Shimerda, who faced snowstorms and strayed cattle, rough hired-girl's work, desertion, bastardy, and the bearing of many children, all with the attitude that "somehow revealed the meaning of common things," the author undertakes to create, on the same ground as her women stood, a masculine character whom she calls Claude Wheeler.

As if anticipating and condoning the show her hero will make when measured against his feminine predecessors, Miss Cather indirectly remarks that "times have changed"—changed, that is, from the late nineteenth century, when Alexandra, Thea, and Ántonia grew up, to the first decades of the twentieth, when Claude Wheeler reached manhood. Houses and farms have lost individuality; neighbors who used to be friendly are now continually having lawsuits.

But nostalgia—the growth of which the author progressively exhibits in succeeding books—does not explain the weakness of Claude Wheeler; nor does the fact that Miss Cather conceives him as a victim of the

Middle West render plausible his singular ineffectuality.   Claude Wheeler's life is a record of persistent thwarting.   Let the adolescent boy decide to attend the circus, in a car that he has risen before daybreak to wash, and his father announces that some old hides need to be hauled into town, and some filthy-talking hired men be driven along — thus doubly ruining Claude's long-anticipated trip.   Let the youth look forward to college, and his mother, fearing agnosticism at the state university, condemns him to a crudely staffed denominational school.   Let him manage an intramural triumph (an elder brother has prevailed against his trying out for the varsity team), and the unattractive girl at the boarding-house, which his mother has chosen for him, spoils the experience by embracing Claude in public.   Let him finally resolve to attend the state university for special courses, and his father hatches a plan to look after the ranch of a sick friend, leaving Claude in charge of the home place. But if his blood-relatives make him a creature of their own superior wills, his wife humiliates Claude Wheeler even more.

Before his not-unwilling demise, young Wheeler knows a short reprieve.   Although the occasion, World War I, proves so interesting to the author that she all but abandons her hero for documentary material on the American Expeditionary Force, Claude Wheeler manages to show himself in France possessed of a gusto he has never achieved in America.   The land he has come to fight for produces not only beautiful people but beautiful omelettes; and the poplars are gold, the vineyards blue-green, the vine-leaves scarlet. If he cannot give his love to a woman in America, he will have an opportunity in France to exchange his life for the life of a comrade.

But as Claude Wheeler is foiled in his desire to attend the circus, he is foiled in his desire for a sacrificial death. The author mitigates this final act of frustration by explaining that of all delusions which warmed her hero only to chill him, the last—the one for which he died—was the greatest. Not that the folly of war made itself known to Claude Wheeler. At least that much was spared the boy; and his mother was accordingly grateful, because she doubted that he could have borne "that last, desolating disappointment."

In the mother's obituarial musing upon her son is found the crux of Miss Cather's attitude toward her hero. She is very sorry for him. Kissing his girl and finding her unresponsive, he recalls the harshness of the world in general; it is really "too rough a place to get about in." He "wished to God he were sick again." When his wife leaves him for a missionary sister in China, he reflects: "What a hideous world to be born into! Or was it hideous only for him? Everything he touched went wrong under his hand—always had."

Nothing ever went right for Claude Wheeler. Wistful for a pleasing appearance, he invariably bought collars that were too high and neckties that were too loud. At heart an epicure, he lacked good food because of native culinary ineptness; and because of Prohibitionist mania he lacked good wine. His wife's twisted attitude toward sex robbed him of love. Sincerely as he aspired to the aesthetic experience, he met defeat through American contempt for the arts; and as a Protestant, he knew only ugly churches, dull services, and ministers like Brother Weldon. As he concludes shortly before death, nobody ever took the trouble to make a man out of him. He had been born into the world like a bear cub or a bull calf, and so could only paw and upset things, break and destroy.

Within the civilization of America there was no help
for him, and from the civilization of Europe help
came too late.

One of Ours magnifies the limitations of an author
whose fortress is feminism. Containing no vigorous
women (Mrs. Wheeler seems as baffled by life as her
son; while neither Gladys, the girl Claude should have
married, nor Enid, his wife, shows any substance),
this book reads as depressingly as a possible version of
O Pioneers! with Carl Linstrum in the principal role
or *The Song of the Lark* sustained by the voice of
Fred Ottenburg.

4

A Lost Lady (1923) may be regarded as stepping-
stone between the two types of novel which Willa
Cather successively attempted. *Alexander's Bridge,*
the pioneer trilogy, and *One of Ours* rank as biographical novels; while from *My Mortal Enemy* on-
ward, Willa Cather identifies herself with the belletristic school of fiction. *A Lost Lady* marks her last
successful attempt to integrate a story around a central
character. But even this book, with its division of
interest between Neil Herbert, the narrator, and Marian
Forrester, the heroine, emphasizes a tendency toward
diffusion already apparent in the author's earlier work.
O Pioneers! breaks sharply in the middle, with the
first half given over to the conquest of the land by
Alexandra Bergson, the second to the fatal love of
Marie Tovesky Shabata. *The Song of the Lark* contains large blocks of unassimilated material on Mexican folkways and cliff-dweller anthropology. *My
Ántonia* becomes at times hardly more than a collection of sketches, with the name character temporarily
displaced by such a personage as Tiny Soderball, who
struck it rich in Alaska, or by a crippled Negro, who

found himself through the piano keyboard. But these novels all achieve a species of unity; it is an organic unity, stemming from the feminine personality at core. Although similarly biographical, *One of Ours*, fashioned around a masculine character, appears a looser fabric even than *My Ántonia*. It is the dominating desire of its heroine which binds each novel of the pioneer trilogy. Alexandra Bergson wants to farm successfully (Marie Shabata wants Emil Bergson); Thea wants to sing in grand opera; Ántonia wants to love and bear children. Claude Wheeler's wishes are as fluid as his will. Through the irresolution of its hero, *One of Ours* vapors away in an ambiguous arraignment of American civilization. Deprived of a coördinating feminine personality, a story by Willa Cather tends to become a series of episodes.

But although the personality of Marian Forrester, the unfaithful wife of an infirm retired railroad contractor, cannot hold *A Lost Lady* quite together, the division of interest between the heroine and the narrator of this novelette finds compensation, for many critics, in a belletristic element, notable for the first time in the fiction of Willa Cather. By its title, *A Lost Lady* indicates the author's intention to follow the biographical pattern of her earlier writing; and, admittedly, whatever power, other than evil, inheres in this slight tale is contributed by the charming Marian Forrester. Against Frank Ellinger, who has the look of a man who could bite through iron, and Ivy Peters, the bird-mangling boy who grows up to be an unscrupulous lawyer,—against these labelled villains, Neil Herbert, the chivalrous witness of the story, and Captain Forrester, the deceived husband, together make a small enough show. But even granting the beauty, grace, and social virtuosity of Mrs.

Forrester, *A Lost Lady* announces a shift on the part of the author from emphasis on story-telling and character delineation to a concern for style and polished imagery more requisite to *belles lettres* than out-and-out fiction.

The second novelette of this period, *My Mortal Enemy* (1926) shows even greater elaboration of aesthetic detail than *A Lost Lady*. Vignettes on religion, opera, poetry, and the drama appear as a succession of exquisitely embroidered screens behind the gaunt action of the center stage. Myra Driscoll Henshawe, an Irish Catholic heiress, defies her great-uncle to marry the son of an Ulster Protestant, regrets her bargain, and pays out her husband with shrewishness the rest of her days. Like the majority of Cather heroines, Myra Henshawe absorbs whatever force there is in the story, leaving Oswald Henshawe to vague unrealized potentialities. "In another sort of world" Oswald's powers "might have asserted themselves brilliantly"; meanwhile, within this world, Myra Henshawe manages to cover herself with "brilliant wrappings." Or, to state the case more generally, woman's achievement is demonstrable; man's continues in the realm of hypothesis. But *My Mortal Enemy* wears such a rich cloak that the underlying feminism almost loses itself in a meditation on the fine arts.

5

Between the writing of her two novelettes, the author had already testified to her evaluation of the aesthetic experience. Napoleon Godfrey St. Peter, Miss Cather's protagonist in *The Professor's House* (1925), is convinced that art-religion has given man his only happiness. As Claude Wheeler mourned the generation of his childhood, when neighbors were friends and farmers had been more interested in beauty than in automobiles; as Neil Herbert lamented the passing of the Western pioneer, Professor St. Peter sighs over the end of cathedral building and the rise of science. Yet in *The Professor's House* art-religion serves illusion as war serves it in *One of Ours*. Put a uniform on a boy, send him to France, and he gets the notion that his life is important, his death even more so. Surround a mediaevalist with stained glass, and he believes in a personal God. But end the war, remove the colored windows, and Claude Wheeler or Professor St. Peter will topple over. In the world of such men there is no reality worth either living or dying for; there is only illusion; and in such a world, such men (to use the words of Claude Wheeler's mother) can ill bear disillusion.

When Professor St. Peter, having completed his treatise on Spanish adventurers in America, lies down in the workroom of the old house with the leaky gas stove, he has no more thought of suicide than he has of embezzling. But chance takes its way. His rescue is effected by the St. Peter family seamstress, as good a Roman Catholic as ever plowed through driving rain to early Mass. She has faith; he, only a clinging illusion. Unable to provide him with faith, she opens a window, and sends him staggering back to the new house which, by the very absence of a workroom, reminds him that his time with the Spanish adventurers and the legacy of mediaeval Christianity is over. And the reader, watching the seamstress patch up the professor's life, recalls the mother, patching up Claude Wheeler's death.

The disappointed scholar is hardly more than a mouthpiece for Miss Cather's malediction on the rise of science. Nor does Tom Outland, the other outstanding masculine character, substantiate the author's claim for him as a "many-sided mind, though a simple and straightforward personality." By the time the story opens, the young aviator-inventor has already been killed; the journal which he bequeaths to his teacher, Napoleon Godfrey St. Peter, accomplishes little toward reviving him. The personality of Tom Outland is available chiefly through the medium of the professor's thoughts; and wisps of reverie can hardly restore to life and potency a man long dead.

Yet even if the author had succeeded in presenting a many-sided mind through a simple and straightforward personality, the result would have been almost as unhappy as the case of Claude Wheeler. What glimpses of Outland as are set down reveal another example of persistent thwarting; here is a child who loses his parents, a boy who loses his friend, a youth who loses his life. And posthumously, Tom Outland's reward is the same: his patents enrich the man who has married the inventor's fiancé.

The author's sympathy for both St. Peter and Outland is fairly palpable. Teacher and pupil, they were deserving men; but somehow fate, in a Willa Cather novel, bestows victory only upon deserving women characters.

The Professor's House contains no feminine character fit for the laurel. And because it lacks an integrating feminine personality, it fails of unity. Tom Outland's journal refuses to assimilate with the rest of the narrative not only because of its disproportionate length, but because of its technical subject matter, variously divided between railroading, archeology, and ethnography. Moreover, there is a confusion of themes in the novel; the cause of art-religion advanced by St. Peter blurs out under the scientific researches of his pupil.   But the book offers nice imaginery, a pleasant tribute to mediaeval craft and ceremonial, and, by way of condiment, a gibe at modern creature-comfort civilization.

Death Comes for the Archbishop (1927), the author's next full-length piece after *The Professor's House*, finds a greater concentration on style than manifested in any preceding work and a structural looseness so marked as to place it almost outside the genre of the novel.   Always painted as with the brush of a superb water-colorist, the scene moves from the Sabine Hills of Italy to the American Rocky Mountains, hovering for a period in the Middle West and advancing toward the Pacific Coast, blending in progress such diverse elements as a desert setting and epicurean interest in food, Navajo repatriation and French architecture of the Midi Romanesque school.   There is neither central character nor central theme.   Women scarcely appear in this series of episodes, which the author attempts to unify through the person of Father Latour.

Jean Marie Latour has been cited by several critics, notably René Rapin, as proof of Miss Cather's ability to draw male character.   Granting the inadequacy of her previous masculine portraits, such commentators signal the Archbishop as a summit in the development of a creative artist.

To the present reviewer, the character of Jean Marie Latour is like a temple dedicated to a cult over which dissension has ceased. The author sets him up as a good man; sets him up. For he is a literary puppet, static in his goodness, removed except by proxy from the strife of human attainment.   Only from without does evil encroach upon Father Latour.   Buck Scales pillages and murders; Friar Baltazar becomes a tyrant instead of a shepherd to his parish; Padre Martinez parades his mistresses; Father Lucero squeezes out the last gold coin from his peons: but never is the Bishop called to kneel for his own sins. Or is it a sin to become impatient with Father Vaillant, when that friend and former seminary-mate is slow in deciding to leave France for America? Recollection of that unquiet moment is all that disturbs Bishop Latour in old age, as apparently the sole blemish upon a long and otherwise faultless life. Not for Jean Marie Latour to cry out: "That which I would, I do not; that which I would not, I do, I, chief of sinners!" Unlike such historical saints as Paul of Tarsus or Blaise Pascal, Father Latour has no need of penitential prayer or iron wristlets. His sanctity is not only ready-made, it fits every occasion.

Depriving Latour of the right to struggle for his own measure of divinity, Miss Cather constructs a lay figure which neither vestments nor liturgy can quicken. The emptiness of the Bishop's role, even in a book where *Death* begins the title, reveals itself the more insistently whenever a woman joins the *dramatis personae*. Let the narration turn, however indirectly, upon Magdalena Valdez, whose husband, Buck Scales, has killed each of their three children, in a manner too horrible to relate; or upon the charwoman, Sada, held in slavery by an American family: and the mortuary calm of the novel vanishes. Only through the appearance of a feminine character does this story emerge from a mild sweetish reverie on the old Southwest, in which even Kit Carson turns out a perfect gentleman.

Shadows on the Rock (1931) tells of a priest for whom spiritual attainment is more difficult than for

Father Latour. Although Noël Chabanel, a scholar and teacher of the French seminaries, dedicated his life to the Huron Indians, he continued to despise their mode of life, to find their language impossible of mastery, and to feel himself cut off not only from the love of his charges but from the love of God. And if Noël Chabanel offers a case of mistaken religiosity—granted that it was mistaken—such misdirection is not confined within *Shadows on the Rock* to one sex alone. Again raising doubts as to the acceptability of human sacrifice, Miss Cather presents a short biography of Jeanne le Ber, the richest heiress in Canada, who immured herself in a convent cell, to receive not peace but despair.

The apparent rejection by God of those who seek to serve Him is however scarcely the main theme of *Shadows on the Rock.* Like several predecessors, this book develops not by main-stream narration, with carefully subordinated tributaries, but by anecdote and character sketch, each as interesting as the next. Willa Cather has the power, rare enough, of infusing incidents and people with such vitality as to make the reader fairly exclaim. But what these memorable episodes, these lifelike persons, bend toward, what they mean in totality, is not easy to recognize. *Shadows on the Rock* seems to be another of the author's commentaries on immigrant adjustment to a new land. Here the land is seventeenth-century Quebec, and no research has been spared to recreate the time, the place, and the inhabitants. Yet it is not the scholar but the artist who triumphs in these pages, where by some never-to-be analyzed magic, a vanished world knows rebirth.

In this re-creation Apothecary Auclair, devoted to the governor-general of Canada but dissatisfied with the King, Louis XIV, plays a part; so do the old Bishop and the new, M. l'Ancien beggaring himself to maintain his charities, while his young successor builds an episcopal palace that must be reached by twenty-four steps. And Pierre Charron lends robustness to the tale. Refused by the religious, Jeanne le Ber, he flees to the Northwoods; brave, courteous, and touchingly chivalrous toward his mother, he is preserved from the conventionality of a "Great North Country" romance by a not unamiable cynicism, mostly directed towards nuns and priests. The thirty years' difference between his age and the age of his bride further removes him from the accepted pattern of timberline fiction.

Taken as a group, the masculine characters of *Shadows on the Rock* make good reading, better than good. But if the theme of this novel is the voluntary exile's coming to terms with a new environment, then the woman, as is customary in a novel by Willa Cather, has taken over. It is *la petite* Cécile, twelve-year old daughter of Apothecary Auclair, who carries the burden imposed by her dying mother, the burden imposed upon all pioneer women in Cather fiction by civilization itself.

Tying into the main theme, still another motif links *Shadows on the Rock* with the author's earlier work. The relationship between *la petite* Cécile and the urchin, Jacques, child of a waterfront hussy, recalls the protective attitude of Alexandra toward young Emil in *O Pioneers!*, of Thea toward Thor in *The Song of the Lark*. Sisterly, yet also maternal, the attitude of Cécile toward Jacques returns the reader to *My Ántonia*, where the immigrant girl finds almost a brother in Jim Burden; and to *A Lost Lady*, where

Marian Forrester teaches Neil Herbert much of what he is to learn about the world.

Woman as conservator of civilization, woman as counselor, one function blends well with the other; and in the novels of Willa Cather, there is always a more or less pliant male over whom woman's tutelage shows effect. In the case of Harry Gordon, his preceptress encounters uncommonly stubborn material; Lucy Gayheart has to die before her pupil gains insight; but he does gain it ultimately, and no teacher can ask more.

Lucy Gayheart (1935) presents a triangle of unfamiliar and not-too-intelligible aspect. Each character is reasonable enough, but the significance of their relationship eludes the reader. Yet Lucy's position as donor can be traced out in the piece, and the position of the men as her beneficiaries. Beside the fresh charm of the girl, a charm which lingers after death, the men seem conspicuously unworthy. His enumerated attractions notwithstanding, Clement Sebastian does not climb nimbly into the hero's seat. His broad-shouldered heaviness of person, his melancholy, his boredom, his general out-of-jointness with life win only admiration from Lucy Gayheart; but for the reader Sebastian differentiates himself not too markedly from the myriad misunderstood husbands who seek sympathy at every feminine source. As for Harry Gordon, despite his remorse following Lucy's death, he fits too neatly into the groove of small-town banker. The reader does not forget, any more than Lucy did, that Gordon left his former fiancée to make her way across the city of Chicago without cabfare; the reader does not forget that he left her a second time, to drown in breaking ice.

From the Northwest of her childhood and the Southwest of her maturity, Willa Cather finally returns to her native Virginia, for the locale of *Sapphira and the Slave Girl* (1940). Attempting first to sell the mulatto girl and then to expose her to the lust of her husband's dissolute nephew, Sapphira Dodderidge Colbert should reveal herself as one of the meanest women in fiction. But, unfortunately for reader-ire, Sapphira's meanness, like her husband's piety, comes from afar.

The miller whom the aristocratic Sapphira Dodderidge marries, presumably because at the age of twenty-four she still lacks a husband, Henry Colbert dutifully takes his place among the ranks of the henpecked. Although his act of assertiveness in refusing consent to the sale of his wife's maid places him in a stiffer category than, say, Fred Ottenburg or Claude Wheeler, he remains a background character, for all his forthright principles, his Bible-reading, and consecrated meditation; he remains the miller of Black Creek County, called into action only under the exigency of the plantation's mistress.

6

In the course of twelve novels, Willa Cather has exhibited a feminism both varied and subtle. Almost non-existent in her first novel, *Alexander's Bridge,* which she herself practically disavowed within a decade after publication, the desire to exalt her own sex has provided the essential strength of succeeding works. The pioneer trilogy, on which her reputation will perhaps continue to rest, makes no pretense of sharing the heroic role between the sexes; that part belongs in turn to Alexandra, to Thea, and to Ántonia; and no man may venture near, except to magnify it by his own homage. Even in depicting a light woman, such as Marian Forrester, or a vixen like Myra Henshawe, Miss Cather somehow turns perversity into a Circean symbol, against which Odysseus prevailing earns not approval but disdain. Where no woman dominates the action, a novel by Willa Cather tends to fall into the hopelessness of *One of Ours* or of *The Professor's House;* or to become less a record of human conflict than a series of insubstantial reveries, such as *Death Comes for the Archbishop.* Like her sister-feminists, Edith Wharton and Ellen Glasgow, Miss Cather achieves her literary purpose most effectively in praise of her own sex.

V

FEMININE GAINS THROUGH FEMINIST PORTRAYALS?

IT IS NOW time to assay the losses and gains of feminism as applied to the American novel. The most conspicuous loss results from the treatment of masculine character, which in feminist fiction appears dwarfed and straitened. Whether this loss be deliberately incurred through the desire to magnify the other sex, or whether it stem from the inability of women writers to project masculine character, is of course arguable.

The masculine characterizations of the authors under review will furnish the traditionalist yet another proof of woman's historic failure as an artist. Androgynous mastery of form has always belonged to man. From Praxiteles to Rodin, from Rubens to Renoir, the masculine creator has expressed the feminine psyche as comprehendingly as he has expressed his own. Coloratura arias no less adequately than baritone and bass are written by men. The drama owes as great a debt to Sophocles for Antigone as for Oedipus; and nowhere in his dealing with masculine personality does Euripedes exceed the characterization of Hecuba. If Shakespeare can almost be said to live by his heroines, for Thomas Hardy the qualifying adverb is superfluous. Flaubert may have spoken more truly than he knew in declaring, *Madame Bovary, c'est moi!* Indeed, for the preponderance of masculine novelists, it is the heroine whose name enduringly links itself with that of the author; take away Moll Flanders or Becky Sharp, Clarissa Harlowe or Diana Warwick, and their creators will forfeit perhaps the larger measure of literary distinction.

As for women, either historically or at present, they offer slight evidence of hermaphroditic understanding. Traditionally, woman has done the pretty, delicate thing; and today her apparent weakness in the face of masculine characterization implies continuing limitation. Even so readily recordable a phase of masculine activity as economic occupation seems beyond the powers of the woman novelist.

It has been said that Edith Wharton's stories show men disappearing into a realm of business as unreal as the sheep-herding of the Latin pastorals. Not often does Mrs. Wharton set down details of this idyllic domain; but when, as in the case of *Ethan Frome*, she attempts to particularize about farming or sawmilling, her efforts bring a smile to the lips of a farmer or a sawmill operative. Edith Wharton was a lady of birth, of wealth, and of letters (as Somerset Maugham has none too charitably remarked); yet such triple insulation from the workaday world, through birth, wealth, and the proclivities of a litterateur, did not prevent Count Leo Tolstoi from understanding folk occupations better than did persons who followed them of necessity.

Although Ellen Glasgow touches on the cultivation and manufacture of tobacco, acknowledges the clerical and medical professions and the milder forms of railroading, and, in the story of Nicholas Burr, shows politics as a shaping force, she can hardly be credited with serious attention to masculine labor. Nor does chronic ill health justify the house-riddenness of her viewpoint; Robert Louis Stevenson did much of his writing in bed; Marcel Proust, virtually all there; yet the work of the world emerges from the pages of Stevenson strong as a seaman's rope, and from Proust its absence echoes of deprivation.

Among the three women novelists under discussion, only Willa Cather seems to know the look of the place where a man works.   She follows him behind the riveting hammer and the thresher, into the timberland, the corral, the mill, the caboose; she observes what he is doing, and why.   Critics who sneer at her mystical preoccupation with pots and pans have forgotten the degree to which bridge-building, excavation, the rougher phases of railroading, ranching, and farming have interested her.   Willa Cather knows the size of a man's job, and writes of it as convincingly as if she had held it herself.

Yet the men on the jobs that Miss Cather describes are, of the three novelists reviewed, the most lacking in virility.   Correlation between what a man does and what a man is may well be doubted. Dostoyefsky draws characters innumerable who show no sign of working at all; nor are they morning-coated aristocrats, but men who, the reader infers from their persons, have been battered into shape by the struggle for bread.   And certainly the instances cited— of Edith Wharton and Ellen Glasgow, practically disregarding the occupational factor, as against Willa Cather, who uses it creatively—seem to nullify any apposition between vocation and character.

Nevertheless, the relationship does exist; occupation is a clue to personality.   Viewed from the drawing-room alone, character tends to appear exclusively in terms of sex.   Yet a representation of the human being suffers less from a disregard of occupation than from a disregard of sexuality. Edith Wharton bothers very little about what her men do for a living; they are "society" people, who devote scant energy to market operation, diplomacy, or the law; in the characters of Edith Wharton the acquisitive instinct and the instinct of workmanship are either dormant or extinct; but the sex instinct is neither. Otherwise, the men of her novels would less often show themselves the dupes of women. Ellen Glasgow, slight as is her record of the world which forms men's daily actions, cannot be accused of emasculating her characters. It is Willa Cather who, despite her veracious and exact accounts of masculine affairs, fails to depict a complete male.

Sufficient evidence exists on which to indict the woman novelist with incapacity to handle masculine character; and, on such a basis, to explain the manifestations of feminism in the works of Edith Wharton, Ellen Glasgow, and Willa Cather as involuntary. But before assuming such testimony as conclusive, the critic might profitably examine the aesthetic purpose of Mrs. Wharton, Miss Glasgow, and Miss Cather. Do these writers intend to exhibit masculine personality at its highest, or simply to project it as a foil for a superior woman?

The novels under consideration show a multiplicity of accurately-drawn second-rate male figures, all highly individualized. Indeed *accuracy* as applied to Ellen Glasgow's masculine personages often involves understatement. Oliver Treadwell represents an excellent rendering of the intellectual in surrender to bourgeois standards, as George Birdsong proves himself a thoroughly convincing *homme sensuel*. Among Edith Wharton's heroes Odo Valsecca is a plausible example of the forceless dreamer, while George Darrow

stands out among a host of fictive characters who
accept the world.   In Claude Wheeler, Willa Cather
paints a portrait of frustration so compellingly as to be
recognized by numbers of Americans as truly *One of
Ours;* likewise, many a driven patient husband can be
identified as Oswald Henshawe, many a dissatisfied
artist as Clement Sebastian.   The very prevalence of
substantial secondary masculine figures in their novels
raises the question whether Edith Wharton, Ellen
Glasgow, and Willa Cather do not deliberately assign
pre-eminence to their own sex, under conviction that
men are unworthy of first rank.

In the stories of Mrs. Wharton, men are condemned
for their paucity of understanding.   The lament which
sounds from Mrs. Wharton's fiction is not that
woman must inhabit a man's world, but that, because
of man's unperceptiveness, each sex is consigned to a
different world.   Mrs. Wharton would be the last to
assert, with Browning, that souls may lie closer than
bodies.   "They may," the reader of a Wharton novel
fancies the author conceding; "but I have never seen a
case in point."   Men are the visitors who never arrive.   Women wait for them their life long, women
who demand neither the vote nor economic equality,
women who seldom clamor for a single standard of
sex morals.   What the women of Edith Wharton's
novels crave is an understanding presence, and that,
man is never able to accord.   The barrier of sex is for
him always insurmountable; woman can peer around
it to make out what manner of being he is; but for
the man of Edith Wharton's conceiving, woman is
always walled away, by his own blindness; so that
she, unbeheld, finally ceases to behold, continuing on
in her drawing-room, like the first Mrs. Leath, dead

and yet unburied, memorialized in an attitude of vain expectation.

It is not for understanding that the women of Ellen Glasgow's novels cry out. The mechanism of the masculine psyche is so plain that any search on their part for sympathetic communion would be gratuitous. A Glasgow heroine not infrequently feels that if men had been watches, she could take "them apart, and put them together again without suspending for a minute the monotonous regularity of their works."

But despite the fact that men are, as Ellen Glasgow views them, mere mechanical constructs, they manage to exert life-long tyranny over women. "The truth is," declared Sara Haardt, "Ellen Glasgow views all women as inevitably oppressed and tragic." Dorothea Lawrence Mann found Miss Glasgow very sorry for women, and correspondingly unsympathetic toward men; while James Branch Cabell designated the dominant theme of his fellow-Virginian as the tragedy of Everywoman, lately enacted in the Southern States of America. "Ellen Glasgow has depicted Southern women, and in some sort all women, as the predestined victims of male chivalry."

Miss Glasgow spent many years not only in championing the intellectual freedom of women, but in trying to deliver her sex from the bondage of love. The celestial variety, imposed through religion, was responsible for the most galling fetters. Like Lenin reviewing the position of the Russian masses under Greek Orthodoxy, Ellen Glasgow looked back upon the Southern female chattel as under dominion of primarily the Protestant Episcopal Church. Nothing else could have kept women in their place generation after generation; nothing but the church could have

made them accept with meekness the wing of the
chicken and the double standard of sex morals.

If the fiction of Ellen Glasgow pictures woman as
struggling against traditional oppression, the Cather
stories assume woman's dominance as pre-established.
The heroine of a novel by Willa Cather has no need
to do battle against an impressionable and sentimental
youth, whose principal characteristics (according to
the critic, Lloyd Morris) are chivalrous aspiration and
impregnable romantic illusion. It is perhaps the in-
herent negligibility of Miss Cather's masculine figures
which best persuades the reader of a voluntary basis
for the treatment of man in a feminist novel.

2

Nevertheless, the exclusion of superior masculine
personality from feminist fiction, by accident or design, constitutes a loss to fiction. The question remains whether this loss is compensated for by a gain
in feminine characterization. Have Edith Wharton,
Ellen Glasgow, and Willa Cather produced studies of
women which surpass those from writers unaffected
by a feminist bias? Has the emphasis of authors like
Mrs. Wharton, Miss Glasgow, and Miss Cather upon
revised political and economic status tended to reveal
woman in a hitherto obscured light?

Ancient literature does not immediately convince
the reader that the feminist novel has increased the
stature of women. The poetry of lands so remote from
Western modernity as Persia and Arabia shows the
female giving a right gallant account of herself, even
in such traditionally masculine pursuits as love-making
and military combat. India, responsible for *purdah*
and the immolation of widows, is also responsible for
the *Mahabharata,* which extols woman as she has been
seldom extolled in any other language than Sanskrit.

The Old Testament, dedicated to Jehovah and the triumph of the masculine principle, offers woman every role that man plays, whether military leader or seer of God. The *Antigone,* product of Periclean Athens and harem seclusion, creates as self-reliant a heroine as any feminist has yet devised.

Throughout the course of literature the masculine writer has not only revealed woman as the companion of man, answerable to God alone, but has repeatedly told off the sins of his own sex. Does Edith Wharton rebel at the double standard? Aeschylus saw the unfairness of it, also; nor did he lend Orestes conviction when the young prince, condemning unchastity in his mother, condoned it in his father. Does Ellen Glasgow decry war as the folly of men invented to torture women? Euripedes put in his word on the subject more than two thousand years ago. Does Willa Cather sigh over women who must endure the men God apportions them? Far more movingly than the American novelist, Nikolai Gogol realized such a situation as it bore upon the Cossack mother in *Taras Bulba.*

But, admittedly, there is a difference between masculine self-indictment and the condemnation of men by women. Masculine artists have shown man as somehow worthy of the anguish woman suffers on his account; they have argued that if man deprives woman, he also dowers her, and that the relationship between the sexes is reciprocal.

The mutuality of the sexual relationship is seldom admitted by a woman writer. She sees her own sex as bestowing, the other as ungratefully or negligently receiving. The fact that man and woman come together for life—and not alone for the life of the unborn—is implicitly denied by Ellen Glasgow and

Willa Cather, and by Edith Wharton but grudgingly admitted.

Yet despite the earnestness of their claim with regard to self-sufficient femininity, not one of these novelists has exceeded, or even seriously challenged, the great portraits of women drawn by masculine writers who had no desire to deprecate either half of the human race.   Ellen Glasgow once wrote a book called *The Wheel of Life,* in which the heroine dazzles an admirer by sheer force of mind.   "He had never before met a woman of commanding intellect," the author cannot forbear to remark.   But the reader doubts that the admirer had met one then, even feels a little sorry for the man, listening to the pertness of Laura Wilde when he might have been companioned by Diana Warwick.

Ántonia Shimerda has been praised as a monument to American literature.   And perhaps she is, to American literature.   But literary achievement must be judged before an international tribunal; and an impartial critic, saluting Ántonia's fecundity and praising her feminine exuberance both in girlhood and in hard-driven middle-age, can nevertheless hardly fail to recall that, a full decade before Willa Cather was born, a certain Russian ex-soldier had created a girl of much laughter and full breasts, and (to quote Ávram Yarmolinsky) through her had established *War and Peace* as a chronicle not of the battlefield but of the family, with its ensign not a flag but a diaper— "stained yellow instead of green."   The name of this girl was Natasha; the daughter of a count, she married a prince; but the quality of her motherhood is such that she speaks—through her masculine creator—for every peasant woman who has held a child in her arms.

3

The shrinkage of masculine personality in feminist fiction, unintentionally or by design, appears to have produced no corresponding extension in the stature of woman; nor has woman received a more notable championship from her avowed defenders than from writers seeking to envision life in its wholeness. The long view of literature, then, renders the effects of feminism almost entirely negative.

Examined, however, in the narrower and more immediate light of the modern American novel, feminism may be seen as the conservator, if not the creator, of certain positive literary values. A consideration of such values will occupy the following chapter.

VI

FEMININE *versus* MASCULINE HUMANISM

CATHER	—	DREISER
GLASGOW	—	FAULKNER
WHARTON	—	WOLFE

THE CONTEMPORARY American novel is, broadly speaking, a product of humanism. Within this general classification, it splits up into special aspects, variously identified as romanticism, realism, naturism. But despite minor diversities, these secondary *isms* all converge in point-of-view, each rejecting, like the humanism from which they spring, a concern with the otherworldly, or what the religionist terms the divine, element in mortal affairs. Observed through humanist eyes, man is no divided creature, half-animal, half-god, eternally teetering between two worlds, at home in neither. Man has an abiding place, peculiarly shaped to his own needs, human needs all; and in this realm, equally untenable by god or beast, he encounters his own problems, human problems all, which he solves with such success as his own powers, unaided, may yield.

Ideally, this is the situation as the humanist offers it to the writer of fiction, man essentially separate and defined. Yet, however orthodox a humanist the writer of fiction may declare himself, and however sincerely he may be committed to the distinction of man from the animals beneath and the gods above, he cannot escape the requirements of his own craft, which demands primarily a machinery of conflict.

For the writer within the religious canon, this machinery is an inherited possession. Whether its dogma be original sin or metempsychosis, religion stamps man as both protagonist and antagonist, an arena within himself, and most rebelliously a dweller upon earth. But the humanist writer of fiction, limiting man's abode and seeking to present him as satisfied with this limitation, must provide a different type of struggle from that which rends the god-beast of religious conception. He must show man content with his human status and neither falling below nor aspiring above, yet engaged in opposing some force worthy of himself.

Such opposition has been provided, both in the case of the realist and the romantic schools, by organized society. Man, good as an individual, somehow absorbs and spreads contamination through group living. This is the thesis of a realist like Theodore Dreiser and of a romantic like Thomas Wolfe. Yet society, its bulk notwithstanding, tends to seem insufficient as a dramatic obstacle, and by its insufficiency sets both realist and romantic to searching for a suitable adversary. Having rejected the religious hypothesis, which assumes man as simultaneously divine and imperfect, the humanist writer of fiction can hardly avoid another form of dualism: that which apprehends character at both human and subhuman levels. Indeed, the more humanistic the novelist's approach, the more apparent the dualism; within the novels of Henry James, animal behavior breaks harshly upon the preponderantly human proclivities of his characters; only when humanism has spent itself in the naturism of Ernest Hemingway or William Faulkner does the literary transaction again appear to take place on a single plane, the level of animal behavior.

The difficulty of maintaining action on one plane besets women writers less than men; for whereas the masculine humanist arranges his fiction around generic man, the feminine writer is prone to consider man with sexual specificity, visualizing him as the fixed opponent, if not the actual enemy, of woman. For the feminine novelist, life defines itself less often as a conflict between the individual and society than as a struggle between the sexes. Instead of assigning generic man the focal point, the woman novelist places her own sex at the center of contemplation; and unlike her masculine contemporaries, who, despite their philosophy, continually stray down to animal levels in search of an antagonist, the feminist writer continues firmly in the way of humanism.

2

Perhaps because they considered him worthy of their antagonism, the feminists have presented man with a dignity denied by his own sex. Even at its bitterest, feminist fiction never describes the human male as the end-product of slum situations, or a creature peculiarly given to incest and inversion, or yet merely a fighting-and-lusting animal. And when she temporarily leaves off baiting him, the woman novelist gives an account of her millenial enemy in much closer accord with the traditional rendering than is to be found in contemporary fiction by men.

Both Willa Cather and Theodore Dreiser wrote an American tragedy, and within a short time of each other, Miss Cather publishing *One of Ours* in 1922, Dreiser following three years later. Through their respective protagonists, Claude Wheeler and Clyde Griffiths, both novelists ask the same question: can an individual exercise his potential in the modern world?

In answering that question, *One of Ours* reveals a range of values beyond the cognizance of *An American Tragedy*. Claude seeks cultivated companionship and appreciation of the arts; Clyde aims hardly higher than a big car and an easy way with women. Claude dreams of love and understanding; Clyde asks only an opportunity to combine social and sexual indulgence. *An American Tragedy* presents man as resolvable into primitive appetites, his morality the result of shifting chemisms, his religious impulses explicable in terms of constitutional weakness or unrecognized hankering after social approval. Desire for social approval is, in fact, the distinguishingly human characteristic of the Dreiser hero; otherwise, he is simply an animal, without humor and without taste; an animal in search of food, shelter, and sexual gratification. *One of Ours* portrays a being of moral sense, cerebral capacity, emotional outreach. Although equally persuaded as to the futility of human endeavor, Willa Cather and Theodore Dreiser nevertheless arrive at different conclusions regarding human personality. By the quality of her protagonist's seeking, Miss Cather establishes relationship with those writers who have seen humanity as a vehicle of the spirit.

The same can be said of Ellen Glasgow, in her characterization of Nicholas Burr. Qualified by more differences than points in common, Miss Glasgow's *The Voice of the People* and the *Absolom, Absolom!* of William Faulkner, present the same theme: the desire to rise in the world; more specifically, the desire of an ill-born Southern boy to meet his superiors at ease. Faulkner selects a time some years before the Civil War

and afterwards; Ellen Glasgow, the period of recon-
struction.

At first glance, *The Voice of the People* seems
atypical of the author, in that it chooses for protagonist a masculine character; but analysis reveals similar-
ity of motivation behind, say, *Barren Ground,* as feminist fiction as Miss Glasgow ever composed, and the
story of Nicholas Burr, which lauds a male being. Both
novels propose the same query: can a member of a
long-oppressed group free himself (or herself) from
the weight of tradition? The author's reply is a reso-
lute, though conditioned, affirmative. The son of a
peanut-farmer may become governor of Virginia (a
betrayed woman may live to watch, from her own
ample acreage, a former lover being carted off to the
poorhouse) ; but ascent will be grim, and at the summit the climber will be acclaimed by death.

But not by death alone. That is the essential difference between Miss Glasgow's novel and William
Faulkner's. Nicholas Burr fights his way past Vir-
ginian snobbery not merely that his girl may marry
a rival or that his body may cool a lynching frenzy.
Eugenia Battle does marry a man of her own class; a
mobster's bullet does kill Nicholas Burr: but these incidents occur by the way. What Burr has set out to
accomplish, he accomplishes. Freeing himself from
the enslavement of the soil and from the prejudices of
those who consider themselves his betters, he fulfills
his own powers as he recognizes them.

The powers of Thomas Sutpen in *Absolom,
Absolom!* are not easy to define. The whole novel is
written with dark indirection, as if the literary material
involved would not bear full scrutiny. There is a
hoarse whispering about Sutpen's attitude toward his
first wife and toward his servant, about Sutpen's pro-

posal to Miss Rosa Coldfield, about his relations with
Wash Jones's granddaughter; everything is said out of
the side of the author's mouth, in fear perhaps of los-
ing audience should the bogey-man pitch be abandoned.

For despite the sepulchral muttering, little seems
in pain of articulation. *Absolom, Absolom!* is no
Southern apologist's cry for a day that is done; or
Sutpen during his struggle for place would have discovered other than a snob's values in a stratified sys-
tem of caste. *Absolom, Absolom!* is no plea for im-
proved race relations between Southern whites and
Southern blacks; or the author's portraits of mulattoes
and darker folk would be limned with sympathy.
Absolom, Absolom! is no brief for the Southern poor
white; or Wash Jones and his granddaughter would
earn more than a shudder. But on behalf of its protagonist, Thomas Sutpen, *Absolom, Absolom!* has even
less to say than for the classes which serve to define him.
There is no substance to the man, but only a drawn-
out unpleasantness, due more to the author's convulsed
syntax than to any actual telling-off of evil. Sutpen's
existence seems to devolve upon a single desire, that
which inheres in all organic matter, the desire to continue life, either in original form or through generation. Drunkenness, arrogance, and cold lechery notwithstanding, Sutpen appears less a human being than
a personification of that mindless energy which is
observable all over the earth, but more spectacularly
in jungle lands, where incipient life and advanced decay
proceed together. As for the problem originally pro-
posed, that of hoisting oneself by one's own boot-
straps, such a performance is shown in Sutpen's case
as ringed around with folly, since the author makes
clear that no feat of elevation would be sufficient to
surmount chaos. *Absolom, Absolom!* offers an ex-

ample of naturism as pure as could be sought, an identification of man with the surrounding overgrowth in
a brotherhood where all breeds find a common doom.

William Faulkner's novel, then, by no means du-
plicates the central portraiture in *The Voice of the
People*. Like one of those monsters evoked by the
early mythology of a race, Sutpen returns after six
unhappy decades to the murk whence he was conjured.
But Nicholas Burr is recognizably a man, and a man
who struggled to some purpose. Even the woman
who rejected him in youth concedes his life's attainment, nor can his successful rival hold back praise,
"He was a great man!" In developing a theme of human aspiration, the feminist, Ellen Glasgow, pays far
higher tribute to masculine personality than can be
read in the pages of William Faulkner.

The Valley of Decision, Edith Wharton's first
novel, sets its hero on a two-volume progress in a
manner which might profitably be compared with the
quest begun in Thomas Wolfe's first novel, *Look
Homeward, Angel*, and terminated in *Of Time and the
River*. The background neither of Thomas Wolfe's
story nor of Mrs. Wharton's is accidental. Although
Rome echoes dimly in the eighteenth-century chronicle
of the Po Valley, the very reverberations of its name
establish a continuity of three thousand years. And
there are other cities, of lesser antiquity than Rome,
but not *parvenu* merely, Venice, Genoa, Milan, Turin,
which remind the hero that his own life-span is
scarcely the measure of time. The hero of *Look Homeward, Angel*, on the contrary, watches a city parallel
his own growth. Surrounding his hometown, to be
sure, is the older South; but the tradition of this region Eugene Gant ignores or despises. Even as a
freshman he saw through the platitudinous pedagogy

on Pulpit Hill; and he was hardly out of the primary department at Sunday School when the snubs of better-placed children showed him religion for what it was.

Odo Valsecca stands humbly in the presence of secular wisdom, and as a follower of the Church he devoutly kneels. Not that the indurability of tradition escapes him, nor the need of each generation to set out afresh for Delphi. And certainly he has more to remember against institutionalized Christianity than the snubs of small children. He has witnessed its contrived miracles at first hand; he knows its debauchery, greed, and tyrannical misuse of power. But for Valsecca these are all corporeal, and therefore transitory, blemishes upon the real, the mystical, Church.

As Odo accepts traditional piety, he likewise accepts his parents. He does not misprize his father for shirking parental duty in a puppet's role at court, his mother for putting him at the foot of her private concerns. But Eugene resents the elder Gants as he resents the constraint of religion and formal education. He must free himself from his parents or be devoured; in his father and mother he recognizes nothing except a threat to his own individuality.

Differing in filial attitude, Mrs. Wharton's hero and Thomas Wolfe's also differ in their attitude toward sex. For the young Italian, love is never a gesture like any other; even at its most trivial, it marks out meaning. For young Gant sex proceeds on a strictly commercial basis until the dream-made-flesh breaks through the money-changing pattern, immediately to land Eugene at the Celestial City. Perhaps because sex in the life of Odo Valsecca is constantly significant, it is not finally significant. He does not delude himself about the possibility of attaining ulti-

mate happiness through human love.   As he acknowledges father and mother, he likewise acknowledges his
spiritual antecedents.   A son of his parents, of his race,
and of his God, Mrs. Wharton's hero forms an interesting contrast with the virtually self-engendered hero
of Thomas Wolfe.

3

Through the characterization of Odo Valsecca, as
a being at once imperfect and divine, *The Valley of
Decision* seems to defy the canon of humanism and
link itself with the literature of spiritual quest.   Yet
the tenuity of such an alliance becomes apparent as
soon as Mrs. Wharton's first novel is placed beside a
book like *Pilgrim's Progress*.   Bunyan's allegory is a
document of the soul; Mrs. Wharton's novel treats of
the person, the charming handsome person of an eighteenth century monarch.   It is a description not of
celestial mansions but of eighteenth century architecture; and although this architecture includes cathedral
as well as palace, every building which Odo Valsecca
looks upon is made with hands.   And so is the reigning duke himself.   Let the author picture his divided
nature as persistently as she will, whatever reality he
encompasses is of earth.   *The Valley of Decision* contains no Interpreter's House, no Mount Zion.   Compared with Christian, Odo offers more points of difference than when compared with Eugene Gant.

For Edith Wharton is not a searcher of souls. This
fact she realized herself, and after *The Valley of Decision* steadfastly continued the investigation of minds
and bodies.   Her first novel is a mere retrospect toward
another age; after this initial experiment, she became of
the twentieth century, hardly less than Thomas Wolfe.
Any scrutiny of writers who have attempted to picture
man as an aspect of divinity will result in placing both

Mrs. Wharton and Thomas Wolfe among novelists concerned with the terrestrial domain of the human creature.

A previous section of this study attempted to point out significant differences between Nick Burr in *The Voice of the People* and Thomas Sutpen in *Absolom, Absolom!* These differences tend to remain even after both novels have been set beneath the portrait of a third self-made man, the David of *I Samuel* and *II Samuel*, of *I Kings, I Chronicles,* and the *Psalms.* Just as William Faulkner drew upon the Bible for his title, he drew upon the Bible for his narrative structure, telling the story of his dynast from five different points-of-view (author, Rosa Coldfield, Quentin, Quentin's father, Quentin's grandfather). Perhaps *Absolom, Absolom!* is intended as a parody upon dynastic ambition; Mr. Faulkner appears to grimace during his inversion of the Davidic legend. Instead of begetting a line who maintain unbroken royal succession, son following father on the throne of Judah over a period of four hundred years, Thomas Sutpen looks upon posterity through the person of a Cretin negroid. Instead of being given a king's daughter to wife, Sutpen marries a woman brushed with tar. Instead of dying in a "good old age, full of days, riches, and honour," Sutpen sprawls in his own blood at the hovel of Wash Jones.

But if, in shaping his David, Mr. Faulkner uses symbols more appropriate to mysticism of the lower path than to the philosophy of the Twenty-third Psalm, Miss Glasgow, for her part, draws on no element inconsistent with a common sense approach to literature. Even Nicholas Burr, who signifies in personal achievement more than any other character she ever created, calls on nothing beyond himself. The religious postulate, that man has access to power which enables him to transcend mortal limitation, is absent both from *Absolom, Absolom!* and from *The Voice of the People.*

Again, if *One of Ours* and *An American Tragedy* be examined in the light of a significant answer to their problem, such as propounded by *Crime and Punishment,* their common relegation of human personality to its temporal phases will vitiate Miss Cather's novel no less than Theodore Dreiser's. Like Claude Wheeler and Clyde Griffiths, Rodion Raskolnikov hungered to test the substance of self. "Freedom and power," the young Russian clamored for; "above all, power! Over all trembling creation and all the antheap!"

Compared with the hero of *Crime and Punishment,* Claude Wheeler loses strength in every area of characterization; the Russian's originality of mind is denied him, the insight into human suffering, the cognizance of supermundane values. Beside Raskolnikov, Clyde Griffiths seems merely a lustful stupid animal.

From first page to last, both Wheeler and Griffiths remain static; whereas Raskolnikov experiences vast spiritual development. The Russian lives to redefine his conception of power and, in large measure, to realize it; the Americans remain in the way of frustration. Wheeler and Griffiths continue to identify evil with society; Raskolnikov recognizes his enemy as himself. The Russian is given penal servitude and hope of new life; Wheeler and Griffiths receive merely death as their portion.

Dostoyefsky's invention is based on religious hypotheses: on belief in the redemptive value of suffering, the forgiveness of sin, the emergence of the Christ within man. In assembling their heroes, both

Miss Cather and Theodore Dreiser severely limit themselves to humanist ingredients, most of which can be
classified either as heredity or environment.   Each of
these elements is unfavorable to human personality;
combined, they extinguish it.   Such is the case alike of
Claude Wheeler and Clyde Griffiths.   Against their
parents and society together, neither young man has
a chance.   The pessimism of Miss Cather is hardly to
be distinguished from the pessimism of Theodore
Dreiser.

4

As humanists, then, Edith Wharton, Ellen Glasgow,
and Willa Cather appear unable to raise their own treatment of fictive personality above the contemporary level.
As feminists, their contribution falls measurably below
the great portraits offered to world literature by masculine writers in the past.   This is true even of feminine
characterizations; while with regard to the other sex,
the unwillingness or incapacity of women novelists to
draw superior male figures has pointed toward a biased
view of life as a whole.   Has such an attitude contributed
any positive value whatever, or is it to be regretted as
a blight upon contemporary letters? Answer must await
examination of feminism not only as a point-of-view
but as a way of faith.

VII

THE FAITH OF OUR FEMINISTS

ALTHOUGH more commonly defined as woman's desire for equality or even for supremacy, *feminism* has within this study been regarded as an expression of woman's desire for self-sufficiency. Edith Wharton, Ellen Glasgow, and Willa Cather have shown woman struggling neither to be man's peer nor his master but to exist as an independent entity. Waiving her erotico-maternal function, the feminist heroine has sought absolute achievement, exclusive of sex.

Such an undertaking on the part of fictive woman —not mere emancipation but disjunction from masculinity—is hardly more prodigious than what the actual woman has witnessed in twentieth century America. The magnitude of the experience in her own day and in her own country cannot be appraised without an historical survey of feminine status.

Of all great and vanished societies, Egypt and Sparta made the greatest show of dealing out equality between the sexes. Yet the lower-class Egyptian housewife, discriminated against neither in law court nor marketplace, was the drudge of a machineless age and the victim of her own fertility; the upper-class Egyptian woman served only as a unit in a harem. The Spartan wife, who had the use of her own money and the privilege of marrying two men simultaneously, owed her preferment to the fact that she furnished the chief and basic ingredient of warfare to a civilization which existed as a continuous encampment.

Elsewhere, the ancient woman spent her life in tutelage. During the Golden Age of Pericles, the Athenian wife passed from the *gynaeconitis* of her father to the *gynaeconitis* of her husband, venturing beyond the middle door only in attendance of religious festivals or funerals. At the birth of a daughter, woolen fillets appeared above the portal, to signify the domestic purpose of the infant, as against the olive wreath which proclaimed a male birth. The curriculum for girls in the most enlightened city of antiquity comprised reading, a little writing, and a culling of innocuous songs. Alone of Athenian women, the hetera shared man's educational opportunity and his freedom of movement; but, in return, she surrendered respectability.

In Rome, the woman of good family was answerable to father, husband, or son. As for the double standard, Cato the Censor gave it legal explicitness: "If you were to catch your wife in an act of infidelity, you would kill her with impunity without a trial; but if she were to catch you, she would not venture to touch you with her finger, and indeed she has no right." The *pater familias* might also put his wife to death for drinking wine. If, by the end of the Republic, woman was granted the right to sue for divorce, she might still, as late as Nero's reign, be consigned to the adjudication of her husband; and even during the Antonines, feminism was an extraodinary and aristocratic phenomenon. Like Cornelia, daughter of Scipio Africanus and mother of the Gracchi, the Roman woman existed primarily as a link between the generations.

Yet the woman of early Christian centuries had cause to gaze back nostalgically upon vanished pagan rights. For the ascetic spirit of the new religion condemned her sex as the supreme obstacle to sanctity; patristic pens became staves of misogyny, laying upon woman a stripe of disfavor which she bore throughout the Middle Ages, chivalry and the Cult of the Virgin nothwithstanding. Convents, towers, chastity belts, forced and indissoluble marriage went on describing feminine status until the Renaissance; nor did the New Learning contravene the ancient practice of wife-beating.

Indeed, the difference between the woman of the Renaissance and the woman of the twentieth century is a measure of modernity. Although the industrial revolution tended to lessen the physical disparity between the sexes and to lighten burdens peculiarly feminine, the nineteenth century was well elapsed before the American wife had legal remedy for corporal punishment; and in some states several decades of the twentieth century were gone before she could collect her own wages and enter into contracts separately from her husband. Scores of years after the Emancipation Proclamation, she was still picketing for the vote. But when victory came, it came threefold. Almost by a single dispensation, woman secured suffrage, birth control, and twilight sleep. And the while, she continued in America to escape the supreme bane of womankind throughout the ages: numerical redundancy.

Such attainment, unparalleled in the history of civilization, prompts inquiry into a fundamental cause. The twentieth century alone did not bring about this astonishing alteration of feminine status. In twentieth century Islam, womankind remains pretty much as in the days before Mohammed. The Prophet's

admission that both sexes are human did not hinder
the Koran from declaring that rebellious women
should be banished and scourged by their husbands. In
twentieth century China, Japan, India, Ceylon—
wherever the demesne of the Buddha holds fast—feminine status reflects Gautama Siddartha's warning
that it were better to fall into the fierce tiger's mouth
or under the sharp knife of the executioner than to live
with a woman; and understanding femaleness *per se*
as incompatible with Nirvana, she anticipates the highest reward of sanctity as a change of sex during trans-
migrations. In the twentieth century boundaries main-
tained by Confucius, women continue to be distinguished from men as hell is distinguished from heaven;
and in the territory of Manu, women compared with
men are still held to be as created things compared
with gods.

The student of feminine status, then, might not
unreasonably conclude that the position of the modern
American woman owes something to Christianity.
When St. Paul said that there is neither male nor female in Christ Jesus, he was formulating a doctrine
foreign to any other great religious teacher.   Yet it is a
doctrine implicit in the attitude of Jesus toward the
women of the Gospel narrative.

But whereas the teachings of Jesus, working
slowly through the centuries to modify traditional sex
attitudes, gave the feminist her right to speak, they
did not inspire her message.   For feminism is not a
Christian preachment.   On the contrary, in the novels
of Edith Wharton, Ellen Glasgow, and Willa Cather,
it parallels a culminating denial of the Church.

2

Such a statement is apparently contradicted by the
autobiography of Edith Wharton, who in *A Backward*

Glance professes complete accord with Protestant Episcopalianism.   To the Church of England, little changed under its American name, New Yorkers of her childhood memory probably owed their superior suavity and tolerance.   Spared the fissiparous tendency of the Protestant sects, and the sanguinary evangelism which harrowed New England, Episcopalian New Yorkers distinguished themselves from the children of the *Mayflower* by their milder manners, greater love of ease, and franker interest in money and good food. To Anglicanism, the author attributes not only her inherited pattern of urbanity but the very words which clothed her speech, early saturated as she was with "the noble cadences of the Book of Common Prayer."

Edith Wharton at seventy-two, seeking to take leave in a well-bred manner, has only praise for her ancestral faith.   And in writing her memoirs she no doubt praised Anglicanism sincerely, as she sincerely declared that she had never had an enemy.   By the time of *A Backward Glance,* the author had reached the amorphous benignity which sometimes characterizes old age. When her values were sharper, Mrs. Wharton acknowledged enemies with relish; they came from every stratum, but most numerously from the mild-mannered, food-and-money-loving New Yorkers, among whom she was born and whom she could never escape, in Europe, in Africa, or at sea.   All this comes out abundantly in her novels.   And despite the names of men she lists in her autobiography, for their sympathetic and valuable criticism of her manuscripts, her fiction denies that she ever entered into a rewarding friendship with a member of the other sex.   It was woman she admired, it was herself she depended upon, because she failed to learn dependence upon that larger self which people of religion call God.

Such is the testimony of her novels, which varies
notably from the crepuscular musings of *A Backward
Glance*. In her autobiography Mrs. Wharton refers
to transplated Anglicanism as a matchless rite; in *The
Old Maid* she speaks of the Episcopal Church as an
edulcorated Church of England, which, under a new
and conciliatory name, left out the coarser allusions of
the marriage service, slid over comminatory passages in
the Athanasian Creed, and otherwise suited itself to
the spirit of compromise "whereon the Ralstons had
built themselves up." The Ralstons were Episcopalians because they recoiled from new religions as they
recoiled from new people; institutional to the core,
they represented a tribe who held new societies together
as seaplants bind the seashore.

Again in *Old New York,* of which *The Old Maid*
is a section, Mr. Raycie, of *False Dawn,* another section, trumpets the virtues of transplanted Anglicanism.
Crying down any puling Methodists or atheistical
Unitarians who might be seated at his laden Episcopal
board, Mr. Raycie inquires of the ladies whether they
had been secretly lending ear to the Baptist ranter at
the end of the lane. No? Well, then, what was the
flutter about the Papists? Granting their heathenish
customs—as Mr. Raycie did, with an oath—the
Papists nevertheless had a real service, didn't they? And
real clergy, too, instead of nondescripts dressed like
laymen, who chatted familiarly with the Almighty in
their own vulgar lingo.

As the Ralstons and the Raycies speak for pros-
perous Episcopalians of the nineteenth century, the
Drovers, of *The Mother's Recompense,* continue the
message of repatriated Anglicanism into the twentieth.
Taking their religion with moderation, the Drovers
and all their kin subscribe handsomely to parochial

charities, invite the rector to a big family dinner once each winter, and count to a nicety the relative social importance of rectors, coadjutors, and bishops.

Nor, according to the same novel, do the Episcopal clergy fail to recognize their own decorative value. The Reverend Doctor Arklow, although he wore pepper-and-salt for traveling, was fastidiously clerical on social occasions; and, in anticipation of becoming co-adjutor, spread his chest to receive the pectoral cross and began making gestures that were full and round, like the sleeves for which they were preparing.

Had Dr. Arklow (eventually Bishop to American expatriates along the Riviera) been contemporary to the Bishop of New York mentioned in *The Age of Innocence,* "the amiable magnificent irreplacable Bishop, so long the pride and ornament of his diocese," the two men would have enjoyed a close camaraderie. But perhaps the most clubbable of all the Wharton ecclesiastics is the vested good-fellow in *Twilight Sleep,* who blends his social presence with Pauline Manford's other distinguished guests, the Cardinal and the Chief Rabbi, to such effect that his hostess wonders why she has strayed from her own creed.

The qualities of the Episcopal Church, sufficient unto the Ralstons and the Raycies, the Drovers and the Manfords, fail the *Bunner Sisters.* During those years when ungrudged industry and whole-minded thrift keep the sisters in decency if not in comfort, they profess allegiance to the most respectable church in America. But when extremity comes, Evalina turns Roman Catholic; and Ann Eliza, although "apostasy had always seemed to her one of the sins from which the pure in heart avert their thoughts," drew no strength from inherited beliefs.

It is through Ann Eliza Bunner that Edith Wharton appears to define her own position with regard to the church. Although she, like the elder Miss Bunner, recoiled from apostasy, Roman Catholicism seemed a steadier vantage from which to take one's sights at life than the church into which she had been baptized. Nowhere in her novels—or in her autobiography — can be found such a tribute to Anglicanism as she renders to Roman Catholicism through Odo Valsecca, in *The Valley of Decision*. According to *The Valley of Decision* the Roman Church represents an ordered beneficence, a simplicity of external life, and a richness and suavity of inner relations, united in a harmony of thought and act. Twenty-three years after the publication of her first novel, Mrs. Wharton describes in *The Mother's Recompense* a similar veneration for the Church of Rome. Kate Clephane yearns for absolution; and her Episcopal rector, Dr. Arklow of the decorative vestments, can only sympathize and deplore, as he tries to shuffle horror out of sight. But those priests of Rome, who speak as impersonal mouthpieces of a mighty Arbitrator— "how different they must be!"

For all her admiration of the Roman Catholic Church, Edith Wharton remained a Protestant; for all her admiration of France, she remained an American citizen—though dying at Brice-Sous-Forêt. Did she recognize a divided loyalty within herself, or is it by chance that the inherited abhorrence of Americans for the Church of Rome echoes through her pages? Adelaide Painter (*The Reef*) was a Bostonian who had lived for thirty years on Gallic soil without altering her reference to the Catholic Church as the Scarlet Woman. Julia Campton (*A Son at the Front*), in spite of her foreign upbringing and continental affinities, remained as implacably and incuriously Protestant as if all her life she had heard the Scarlet Woman denounced from Presbyterian pulpits. Deeper than all her religiosity, deeper than her pride in receiving the Cardinal, deeper than the superficial contradictions and accommodations of a conscience grown elastic from too much use, was Pauline Manford's old Puritan terror of gliding priests and incense and idolatry (*Twilight Sleep*); perhaps that terror was the only solid fiber left in her.

There were many solid fibers in Edith Wharton; but perhaps most solid was her allegiance to good form. Not that she remained a prisoner to custom; in no sense. Even those critics who deny her rank as an artist grant that she broke ground for the plain-speaking tradition of American realism. *The Custom of the Country* has been conceded as opening up the way for Sinclair Lewis, notably in *Babbitt,* and as introducing in the person of Undine Spragg the prototype in American fiction of the international gold-digger. As much she is said to have learned from Henry James, Edith Wharton could on occasion turn teacher, which she did for James in *The Ivory Tower.* Professedly an admirer of Proust, she rejected the stream-of-consciousness as unsuited to her purpose; and for all her desire thoroughly to explore sex motivation, she refused aid from Vienna. And almost alone in her generation she is credited with the sense of tragedy.

Edith Wharton can hardly be accused of following a meek pattern along with her contemporaries, or of producing stereotypic writing under pressure of the past. Yet both past and present reached out to encase her in a mold from which there was no swerving; and in the casting of that mold, the Protestant Episcopal

Church of America contributed restraint, decorum, and
an austere quality of worldliness.   If with her right
hand Mrs. Wharton sought to deny the font from
which she had received baptism, her left hand quietly
resumed its hold; so that, nearing the end of a long life,
she correctly appraised ancestral faith as a shaping influence of her art.

But, after due credit has been rendered the Episcopal Church, there remains unaccounted for the thin in-
transigent flame which illumines the most powerful of
Edith Wharton's writing, that flame which derives
from no doctrine of submission to divine will, as
preached from any pulpit.   It is the burning core of
feminism to be found in the first and last of her fiction, whenever she speaks as one having authority.   It
is the *I*, the peculiarly feminine *I*, the will to triumph
over the masculine obstacle, which gleams in *The Custom of the Country*, in *The Mother's Recompense*, in
The Old Maid, in *New Year's Day*.   The light which
guided the pen of Edith Wharton through fifty-four
published volumes was kindled not by Thomas
Cranmer and Hugh Latimer but by Mary Wollstone-
craft and Susan B. Anthony.

3

The rebellion of Ellen Glasgow against the
Episcopal Church was more insurgent and downright
than any which Edith Wharton ever waged.   Like the
older novelist, Miss Glasgow received the Church by
way of inheritance—from her maternal ancestors, at
any rate, who wandered no further from Anglicanism
than might have been expected of James River Harri-
sons or Randolphs of Roanoke.   But if her mother
represented the Tidewater aristocracy, her father, Francis T. Glasgow, manager of the Tredegar Iron Works,

which supplied the Confederacy with cannon, drew on a Scotch-Irish strain long dedicated to John Calvin and John Knox.   The contention of Anglicanism and Presbyterianism for the soul of the author may be traced over a period of forty years.

A bishop of long residence in Virginia has said that "Miss Glasgow gloried in her unbelief," and Sara Haardt is responsible for the statement that "Her religion, if she can be said to have any, is a kind of philosophy of beauty."   But the writings of Ellen Glasgow testify neither to the vaunting of unbelief nor to the substitution of an aesthetic for religion.   Her novels may be divided into two groups, with *Barren Ground* (1925) as the line of demarcation.   Before *Barren Ground* she leaned toward the faith of her mother; with the publication of her perhaps most famous novel she finally allied herself with Calvinism. Not that the "vein of iron" lacked praise from the author prior to appearance of that specific title, or of the earlier *Barren Ground*.   She had always been her father's daughter as well as her mother's; but for the space of many novels, the Episcopal Church influenced her pen, to reach its climax in *Virginia* (1920).

Not that she openly professed the Church, either through asides in her own voice or more tellingly by the conduct of her characters.   *Phases of an Inferior Planet* (1898) deals with the rejection of the whole Christian doctrine by an Episcopal priest. Yet, in such a light is this rejection presented that the reader may well regard the agnosticism of Father Algarcife as unfortunate.   The Church of the Immaculate Conception, high, celibate, and yearning toward Rome, is shown as a real sanctuary, and its founder, Father Spears, as a saint even to his curate.   It is a rich church, so rich that the music committee can engage a

contralto from the Metropolitan Opera House to assist
in the celebration of the Easter Mass; it is a very rich
church; but unlike St. Stephen's or St. Matthew's or
Grace Church in the novels of Edith Wharton, it is
not empty.   Metropolitan box-holders looked to the
rector for guidance as slum-dwellers looked to him;
and if Anthony Algarcife failed them it was because of
his own unbelief.

Of all the Episcopal clergy in the early novels of
Ellen Glasgow, only Father Algarcife reveals his
doubts.   The rector of *The Battle-Ground* (1902)
ministered to the squierarchy in jovial accord with
Anglican custom; and Mr. Mullen preached Pauline
doctrine to *Old Church* (1911) with such persuasiveness that at least one lady in the congregation began
to embroider slippers for him.   The Reverend Mr.
Gabriel Pendleton, who removed his cassock only to
assume a Confederate uniform, witnessed by his life
and by the manner of his death the discipleship he had
avowed to Christ; in *Virginia* (1920), the finest book
of the author's first period, the Episcopal Church is
still in the ascendant, with Presbyterianism, as personified by Cyrus Treadwell, running negligibly behind.

Five years later Ellen Glasgow severed literary con-
nection with the church which had fostered the Reverend Mr. Pendleton and his daughter, Virginia.
Barren Ground shows the author renouncing the felic-
ities and amenities culitvated by an emigré aristocracy
in a new land; henceforth, virtue will be made mani-
fest not through feminine toleration of the double
standard and the wing of the chicken but through the
attribute dear alike to Calvinism and Stoicism, the
attribute of courage.   Not that courage, endurance,
grimness of will had gone unextolled in the earlier
novels.   Caroline Meade, of *The Builders* (1919) an-

ticipated Dorinda Oakley when she declared that there must be something one can live on beside love; Gabriella Fowler, name character of the novel published in 1916, wore her chin more conspicuously than her heart; and as far back as *The Battle-Ground* (1902), Betty Ambler showed signs of working her way toward serenity had Dan Montjoy never returned from war.   To point an irreconcilable cleavage between the writing which preceded and followed *Barren Ground* is like trying to set up a final antithesis between Presbyterianism and the Episcopal Church. Some slight overlapping of the two sects must have been detected during the reign of Elizabeth; and in present-day America they are almost indistinguishable. Yet a difference carries over from their conception; and it is on the basis of such a differentiation, slight but fundamental, that the novels earlier and later than *Barren Ground* will be categorized.

That her point-of-view had altered, the author herself realized, as she states in the preface to the edition of *Barren Ground* which appeared in 1933.   In this preface Miss Glasgow asserts that after years of tragedy and the sense of defeat bred by tragedy, she had won her way to the other side of the wilderness, becoming the while a different person.   She regarded the writing of *Barren Ground* "as almost a vehicle of liberation."   From what Miss Glasgow felt herself liberated is not named in the introduction to the novel which offers Dorinda Oakley as the achievement of a quarter-century's struggle.

This achievement was the representation of a human being who had learned to live without joy. Such knowledge had been won by Dorinda Oakley, daughter of good people though not of good family, God-fearing Scotch-Irish Presbyterians, whereas it had been

denied to Virginia Pendleton Treadwell, born to a
lady of the Tidewater and a rector of the Episcopal
Church.   Dorinda's nature had a vein of iron that
"would never completely melt in any furnace."   The
substance of Virginia's being was too fine for mortal
assaying; too fine, the author seems to believe, for
mortal buffeting.   Miss Glasgow will draw no more
Virginias.   Henceforth, her heroines are to live not by
love but by grit.

Although this abandon of the heart in favor of
the chin may not be fairly laid to the espousal of Presbyterianism, nevertheless the author, seeking to give
her new philosophy a name and a face, chose *Vein of
Iron* (1935) as a title, and as its sparse-speeched ex-
ponent appointed Grandmother Fincastle, who lived in
the manse at Ironside, wife of a third generation of
Scottish ministers in America.

But even Grandmother Fincastle, "fortress of
strength" that the author calls her, would not suf-
fice Miss Glasgow, any more than the Calvinism
which had sustained her own paternal ancestors.   In
Vein of Iron appears John Fincastle, whose *God as
Idea* cost him his Presbyterian pulpit.   Apparently,
then, neither Anglicanism nor Calvinism fulfilled the
spirit of Ellen Glasgow.   The Episcopal Church she
found charitable toward every weakness except
thought.   And as a worshipper of intellection, Miss
Glasgow could not, with a good conscience, abide in
an edifice hostile to her god and particularly harsh
toward such of his votaries as happened to be women.

Convinced that the Episcopal Church dispensed an
embalming fluid to devotees of the *status quo*, and
that it could lift only a dead hand to stay the rise of
the middle class and of women, Ellen Glasgow searched
out another faith, one that substituted forthrightness

for urbanity, courage for love. What she won by a shift of emphasis, only she can say. But loftily as she enthroned fortitude, and valiantly as she preserved the determination to write a novel called *Beyond Defeat,* death forced rude entry; nor could the author stifle her last heroine's sigh for a spot where love was over and done with.

Unlike Margaret Fuller, Ellen Glasgow never accepted the universe. Nor did she achieve the patched-up serenity which was Edith Wharton's in old age. By nature a rebel, she found haven neither in the peace between the States nor in an exchange of Anglicanism for the sterner shelter of John Knox. As an editorialized obituary significantly remarks, every major character which Ellen Glasgow created was a figure of rebellion. In her rebellion she was sustained by a faith which owes little to the Christian denominations. The faith which served her as she was best served, over a half-century of literary endeavor, was faith in her own sex.

4

When Willa Cather remarked to Stephen Vincent Benét and Rosemary Benét, "I'm an Episcopalian and a good one, I hope!" she contradicted an impression which many persons received from her books. Critics and lay readers alike, noting the amount of space allotted in her novels to Roman Catholicism, have ranked her—by implication, at least—as other than a Protestant writer.

Now, to be sure, an Episcopalian holds himself as both Protestant and Catholic, but not Roman Catholic; and it is with Roman Catholicism that half of Willa Cather's novels are saturated. The chronology of the non-Romanist half, *Alexander's Bridge* (1912), *The Song of the Lark* (1915), *One of Ours* (1922),

A Lost Lady (1923), *Lucy Gayheart* (1935), *Sapphira and the Slave Girl* (1940), contributes nothing to a hypothesis of cleavage, with resistance to Romanism on one side and inclination toward it on the other. All that can be inferred from inspection of dates is that throughout her literary life Willa Cather showed interest in the Church of Rome.   It may even appear that this interest characterizes her best books— although *The Song of the Lark,* as good a novel as she ever wrote, is a Protestant affair; while, on the other hand, *My Mortal Enemy,* almost her worst effort, contains as large a percentage of Roman material as any item on her list.   *Sapphira and the Slave Girl,* the author's last and poorest book, presents the only full-length Cather portrait of an Episcopalian.

To segregate a shaping faith from the writings of Willa Cather is more difficult than in the case of Edith Wharton or Ellen Glasgow; for although her use of ecclesiastical material is more prodigal than either of the other novelists', Miss Cather might reasonably be ranked as the least religious writer among the three women discussed.   The problem posed by Willa Cather's fiction is essentially aesthetic rather than religious.   Her earliest novel indicated the tendency she followed to the end.   In *Alexander's Bridge,* the name character violated a law of harmony rather than a moral or religious canon—the law of subordination. Trying to juggle two equally agreeable, and opposed, ways of life, Bartley Alexander fell victim to his own formal irresponsibility. And the problem which Alexander failed to solve, the problem of harmonious adjustment, is basic in all of Miss Cather's writing.

For that reason she repeatedly chose the immigrant as protagonist.   Her choice recalls the fury of Joseph Conrad on being accused of writing sea stories.   Con-

rad claimed that he used the sea because it held his
characters where he could observe them: the deck, the
bridge, the wardroom showed people for what they
were.   So does a new country show up people for
what they are, and what it shows most obviously is
a capacity for adjustment.   Willa Cather does not
write pioneer stories.   Even the novel for which she
borrowed a title from Walt Whitman contains no
sweat or labor of tillage.   The concern of Miss Cather
is not with man's struggle to claim a wilderness for
civilization, but rather with woman's success or failure at maintaining effective domestic patterns in an
alien land.   "Alexandra often said that if her mother
were cast upon a desert island, she would thank God
for deliverance, make a garden, and find something to
preserve."   Mme Auclair taught her daughter to keep
clean sheets on the bed and wholesome food on the
table; and, far from France, the Auclair household
prospered.   But Mrs. Shimerda had no gift for home-
making, and her husband on foreign soil committed
suicide.

As Miss Cather selects the aesthetic element of pio-
neering (the various degrees of adjustment effected between new settlers and their environment), she likewise concerns herself with the aesthetic element in ecclesiastical practice.   Her treatment of religion, in the
majority of instances, employs a detached observer,
one who can comment on the scene in possession of
full critical powers, without danger of emotional in-
volvement.   Roman Catholicism in the books of Willa
Cather is most frequently presented through the eyes
of an admiring Protestant.   Emil Bergson looks on the
parish festivities of Amédée Chevalier with ample appreciation of their gusty liveliness, but without desire
to swerve from his own North-European religious tra-

dition.   Although the Shimerdas' preparations for a
Roman Catholic Christmas fairly intrigue Jim Burden,
never far from that young man stands his Baptist
grandfather, spiritually or in the flesh, ready to
Protestantize the whole atmosphere by a bow of his
venerable head.   Professor St. Peter, after having given
his creative years to the study of Spain (convinced
that stained glass provides the best light for illusion)
is eagerly diverted by his Roman Catholic seamstress's
explication of the Magnificat; but that Professor St.
Peter showed other than a scholar's interest is not re-
corded.   Watching John Driscoll's gorgeous funeral,
the Protestant narrator of *My Mortal Enemy* muses
on the possibility of a Roman Catholic soul proceeding
directly from the high altar to the greater glory; but
the question remains pleasantly academic.

Willa Cather traces no internal religious dissension,
presents no protagonist torn by the conflicting claims
of Anglican and Latin Christianity, no series of characters which describe a flight from one Protestant sect to
another.   What the Protestants of Miss Cather's fiction require from the Roman Catholic Church is its
aesthetic element, and that they may take over without charge of apostasy.   And since they receive no more
than they seek, namely, the aesthetic element, they remain for the reader as visitors to the Mass, not as
communicants; they bring to the altar the same respectful, curious, and appreciative glance that is
brought to great museums and opera houses.

As Miss Cather moves further away from the pioneer trilogy, her preoccupation with aesthetics becomes
increasingly evident.   More and more, her fiction re-
sembles a critique by a connoisseur of the fine arts;
and since most of American life—of all life—is unworthy of a connoisseur's taste, most of it in the later

novels is rejected. The reader is invited to meditate on the American past, rather than on its present or future, because from the past one may take what one will. For her most excellent pieces of belletristic writing, Miss Cather choses scenes and times which banish the shrillness of modern civilization: the Southwest before tourists came to Taos and the Quebec of the seventeenth century; places and periods prior to cathedrals of pedagogy, cathedrals of industry, cathedrals of mortuary science.

Yet, however excellent as aesthetic commentary, neither *Death Comes for the Archbishop* nor *Shadows on the Rock*, possesses value as a testament of faith. *Death Comes to the Archbishop* is a series of tableaux, a diorama, which uses Roman Catholic material with such patently spectacular effect as to agitate neither Protestant nor unbeliever. *Shadows on the Rock*, presenting the profoundest religious experience contained in the fiction of Willa Cather, states the case for skepticism not once but twice, in the person of Noël Chabanel and of Jeanne le Ber, with a persuasiveness which might be seriously disturbing were the novel centered upon the relation of man to God. But religion is not the subject of *Shadows on the Rock;* it is (to borrow an expression from Ludwig Lewisohn) the binding; it is the aesthetic solvent through which heterogeneous incidents move toward unity.

Miss Cather has preserved a devotion to aesthetics perhaps unique among American writers of fiction. France may have furnished her counterpart in Marcel Proust, who, like Miss Cather, complements a predilection for the fine arts with sustained treatment of an anomolous sex relationship. But whereas Proust deals with homosexuality, Miss Cather merely points to the unprofitableness of normal association between

the sexes.   In eight of her twelve novels, marriage is
described as not only childless but spiritually sterile.
More rewarding, in the light of Miss Cather's fiction,
is a platonic friendship between a woman and her masculine junior, especially when enriched by appreciation
of the fine arts.

But it is hardly as an expositor of aesthetic asceticism
that Willa Cather has made her contribution to American literature.   Whatever her worth abides in portraits of three heroic women, drawn from her faith as
a feminist.

5

Although constituting the essential strength of
their fiction, feminism eventually failed each of the
novelists here reviewed.   During her last years, Edith
Wharton became increasingly commercial, with power
left only to explore a high-finish technique.   Ellen
Glasgow wrote her final novels in despair; feminism,
pursued to its extremity in *Barren Ground,* showed
her the abyss; and for the rest of her days she was
condemned brackishly to repeat those formulas which
had sustained her militant youth.   Willa Cather, having exhausted the cult of feminism in her pioneer trilogy, set herself toward a godless aestheticism, which
in the hands of a stronger writer would have emanated
a more certain decadence.

A faith which waned during the lifetime of its
most distinguished adherents and which at zenith in-
spired no great literary portraits even of the sex it
undertook to exalt, may feminism yet be credited with
performing any service to American letters?   A valuable service.   By the unequivocal nature of their doctrine, the feminists have illuminated the program common to all contemporary American novelists, male and
female. Feminism is a product of disaffection; so is the

American novel as a whole.   Theodore Dreiser shakes
his fist at chemisms, judgment, and the persistence
of a human concern for the eternal; William Faulkner
smashes out at Appomattox and the invention of the
steam engine; Thomas Wolfe deprecates the apparent
necessity of parents.   But so spacious is his animosity
that the masculine novelist often dissipates his message by sheer vociferation.   The feminist, for her part,
has just one small complaint.   She disapproves of sexuality.   And by limiting her grievance and sharpening
its expression, she has provided a primer for the modern American novel.   This primer of feminist authorship at once reveals what the elaborations of the masculine humanists frequently obscure.   It is the lack
which runs like a portent through all present-day
American fiction; it is the absence of Dante's inscrip-
tion, "In His will is our peace."

EDITH WHARTON

Born into an aristocratic New York family, Edith New-bold Jones Wharton (1862-1937) was educated by private tutors and early given the advantage of foreign travel. She spoke French well enough for Parisians to ask whether she wrote her novels first in their own language and afterwards translated into English. Expert knowledge of German earned her life-long royalties on a translation of Sudermann's *Es lebe das Leben.*

Despite her cultural pursuits, Mrs. Wharton never relinquished the fashionable world. By eleven o'clock she was at home to her friends, having by that time accomplished the daily stint of work which earned her an international literary reputation. *Le Revue des Deux Mondes* published several of her novels, and English literati regarded her as a peer. Appealing to a remarkedly varied public, she was able to see her name simultaneously in women's magazines and in scholarly anthologies of contemporary fiction. One of her early novels, *The House of Mirth,* was adapted for the stage by Clyde Fitch; *The Old Maid* ran successfully as legitimate drama and as a motion picture. During her lifetime Mrs. Wharton published fifty-four titles, including novels, short story collections, critical pieces, travel books, and manuals of interior decoration.

Many honors came to her. In 1920 she was awarded the Pulitzer Prize for *The Age of Innocence;* three years later she received the honorary doctorate in letters from Yale University —the first woman to be so distinguished. The Academy of Arts and Sciences likewise invited her to join an almost exclusively masculine assembly. In 1924 she received the gold medal of the National Institute of Arts and Letters.

Mrs. Wharton spent her last years in France, where she had lived continuously since 1912. Her war work, 1914-1918, drew tributes from Belgium as well as France. Her marriage to Edward Wharton terminated in divorce (1913). She died of a cerebral hemorrhage, in Brice-sous-Forêt.

THE NOVELS:

The Valley of Decision. New York: Scribner's, 1902.
The House of Mirth. New York: Scribner's, 1905.
The Fruit of the Tree. New York: Scribner's, 1907.
Madame de Treymes. New York: Scribner's, 1907.
Ethan Frome. New York: Scribner's, 1911.
The Reef. New York: D. Appleton, 1912.
The Custom of the Country. New York: Scribner's, 1913.
Bunner Sisters, in *Xingu.* New York: Scribner's, 1916.
Summer. New York: D. Appleton, 1917.
The Marne. New York: D. Appleton, 1918.
The Age of Innocence. New York: D. Appleton, 1920.
The Glimpses of the Moon. New York: D. Appleton, 1922.
A Son at the Front. New York: Scribner's, 1923.
False Dawn. New York: D. Appleton, 1924.
The Old Maid. New York: D. Appleton, 1924.
The Spark. New York: D. Appleton, 1924.
New Year's Day. New York: D. Appleton, 1924.
The Mother's Recompense. New York: D. Appleton, 1925.
Twilight Sleep. New York: D. Appleton, 1927.
The Children. New York: D. Appleton, 1928.
Hudson River Bracketed. New York: D. Appleton, 1929.
The Gods Arrive. New York: D. Appleton, 1932.
The Buccaneers. New York: D. Appleton-Century, 1938.

AUTOBIOGRAPHY:

A Backward Glance. New York. D. Appleton-Century, 1934.

ABOUT THE AUTHOR:

Boynton, P. H. *Some Contemporary Americans.* Chicago: University Press, 1924.
Canby, H. S. "Edith Wharton," *Saturday Review of Literature,* XVI (August 21, 1937), 6-7.
*Chanler, Margaret Terry. *Autumn in the Valley.* Boston: Little, Brown, 1936.
Coolidge, Bertha. "Edith Wharton," *Saturday Review of Literature,* IX (July 8, 1933), 614.
Follett, Wilson. "What Edith Wharton Did — and Might Have Done," *New York Times Book Review,* (September 5, 1937), 1.

Hackett, Francis. "Mrs. Wharton's Art," *New Republic*, X (February 10, 1917), 50-52.

Herrick, Robert. "Mrs. Wharton's World," *New Republic*, II (February 13, 1915), 40-42.

Huneker, James. "Three Disagreeable Girls," *Forum*, LII (November, 1914), 165-175.

Kazin, Alfred. "The Lady and the Tiger," *Virginia Quarterly Review*, XVII (January, 1941), 101-111.

*Kunitz, Stanley J. and Haycraft, Howard. *Twentieth Century Authors*. New York: H. H. Wilson, 1942.

*Lovett, Robert Morss. *Edith Wharton*. New York: McBride, 1925.

Lubbock, Percy. "Edith Wharton," *Quarterly Review*, CCXXII (January, 1915), 182-201.

    Portrait of Edith Wharton. New York: D. Appleton-Century, 1947.

*Maugham, W. Somerset. "Give Me a Murder," *Saturday Evening Post*, CCXIII (December 28, 1940), 27.

McCole, C. John. "Some Notes on Edith Wharton," *Catholic World*, CXLVI (January, 1938), 425-429.

*Millet, Fred B. *Contemporary American Authors*. New York: Harcourt, Brace, 1940.

Monroe, N. Elizabeth. *The Novel and Society*. Chapel Hill, N. C. University Press, 1941.

Morley, Christopher. "Edith Wharton's Unfinished Novel," *Saturday Review of Literature*, XVIII (September 24, 1938), 10.

*Overton, Grant. *The Women Who Make Our Novels*. New York: Moffat, Yard, 1918.

Ransom, John Crowe. "Characters and Character," *American Review*, VI (January, 1938), 271-288.

Repplier, Agnes. "Edith Wharton," *Commonweal*, XXIX (November 25, 1938), 125-126.

*Smith, Logan Pearsall. *Unforgotten Years*. Boston: Little, Brown, 1939.

Time, "Edith Wharton," Obituary. XXX (August 23, 1937), 53.

Wilson, Edmund. "Justice to Edith Wharton," *New Republic*, XCV (June 29, 1938), 209-213.

*Contains biographical material.

ELLEN GLASGOW

Ellen Anderson Gholson Glasgow (1874-1945) was born in the house where she died, One Main Street, Richmond, Virginia. A frail child, she was educated at home, teaching herself to read by picking out the letters from Scott's novels. Although barred from the classrooms at the University of Virginia, she secured private instruction and in the course of her career not only became a member of Phi Beta Kappa, but received honorary degrees from the University of North Carolina, the University of Richmond, Duke University, and the College of William and Mary.

Many other distinctions witnessed to her achievement. Publishing at consistent intervals for over a half-century, Miss Glasgow received critical recognition early. Southern commentators often acclaimed her fiction as peculiarly their own; while others found more than national significance. In 1938 the American Academy of Arts and Sciences admitted her to memberhip, and two years later conferred on her the Howells medal for fiction. In 1940 she received the *Saturday Review of Literature* Award for Outstanding Services to American Letters. The following year the Southern Authors' prize came to her, and, finally, in 1942, the Pulitzer Prize for *In This Our Life*. Miss Glasgow's last novel was the selection of a national book club and the basis of a motion picture by the same title.

THE NOVELS:

The Descendant. New York: Harpers, 1897.

Phases of an Inferior Planet. New York: Harpers, 1898.

The Voice of the People. New York: Doubleday, Page, 1900.

The Battle-Ground. Garden City, New York: Doubleday, Page, 1902.

The Deliverance. Garden City, New York: Doubleday, Page, 1905.

The Wheel of Life. Garden City, New York: Doubleday, Page, 1906.

The Ancient Law. Garden City, New York: Doubleday, Page, 1908.

The Romance of a Plain Man. New York: Macmillan, 1909.

The Miller of Old Church. Garden City, New York: Doubleday, Page, 1911.

Life and Gabriella. Garden City, New York: Doubleday, Page, 1918.

The Builders. Garden City, New York: Doubleday, Page, 1919.

Virginia. Garden City, New York: Doubleday, Page, 1920.

One Man in His Time. Garden City, New York: Doubleday, Page, 1922.

Barren Ground. Garden City, New York: Doubleday, Page, 1925.

The Romantic Comedians. Garden City, New York: Doubleday, Page, 1926.

They Stooped to Folly. New York: The Literary Guild, 1929.

The Sheltered Life. Garden City, New York: Doubleday, Doran, 1934.

Vein of Iron. New York: Harcourt, Brace, 1935.

In This Our Life. New York: Harcourt, Brace, 1941.

CRITICAL:

A Certain Measure. New York: Harcourt, Brace, 1943.

ABOUT THE AUTHOR:

Adams, J. Donald, "Virginia Edition Works of Ellen Glasgow," *New York Times Book Review,* December 18, 1938, 1.

Cabell, James Branch. "Two Sides of the Shielded," *Books*, VII (April 20, 1930), 1.

Canby, H. S. "Ellen Glasgow: Ironic Tragedian," *Saturday Review of Literature*, XVIII (September 10, 1938), 3-4, 14.

*"Ellen Glasgow: A Personal Memory," *Saturday Review of Literature*, XXVIII (December 22, 1945), 13.

Cash, W. J. "Literature and the South," *Saturday Review of Literature*, XXIII (December 28, 1940), 3-4.

*Clark, Emily. *Innocence Abroad*. New York: Alfred A. Knopf, 1931.

Cooper, Frederick Tabor. "Representative American Story Tellers," *Bookman*, XXIX (August, 1909), 613-618.

Dabney, Virginius. "A Prophet of the New South," *Books*, V (August 25, 1929), 1.

*Freeman, Douglas. "Ellen Glasgow: Idealist," *Saturday Review of Literature*, XII (August 31, 1935), 11-12.

*Haardt, Sara. "Ellen Glasgow and the South," *Bookman*, LXVI (April, 1929), 133-139.

Jones, H. M. "Ellen Glasgow, Witty, Wise and Civilized," *Books*, XIV (July 24, 1938), 1.

"Product of the Tragic Muse," *Saturday Review of Literature*, XXIII (March 29, 1941), 5-6.

*Kunitz, Stanley J. and Haycraft, Howard. *Twentieth Century Authors*. New York: H. H. Wilson, 1942.

Loveman, Amy. "Ellen Glasgow—A Tribute," *Saturday Review of Literature*, XXVIII (December 1, 1945), 26.

*Mann, Dorothea Lawrence. *Ellen Glasgow*. Garden City, New York: Doubleday, Doran, 1928.

"Ellen Glasgow: Citizen of the World," *Bookman*, LXIV (November, 1926), 265-271.

*Marcosson, Isaac. "The Personal Ellen Glasgow," *Bookman*, XXIX (August, 1909), 619-621.

Mencken, H. L. "A Southern Skeptic," *American Mercury*, XXIX (August, 1933), 504-506.

*Millet, Fred B. *Contemporary American Authors*. New York: Harcourt, Brace, 1940.

Mims, Edwin. "The Social Philosophy of Ellen Glasgow," *Journal of Social Forces*, IV (March, 1926), 495-503.

Murdock, Kenneth. "Folly and the Ironist," *Virginia Quarterly Review*, V (October, 1929), 596-600.

New York Times, November 22, 1945, Editorial.

Overton, Grant. "Miss Glasgow's Arrow," *Bookman,* LXI (May, 1925), 291-296.

*The Women Who Make Our Novels. New York: Moffat, Yard, 1918.

Parker, William R. "Ellen Glasgow: A Gentle Rebel," *English Journal,* XX (March, 1931), 187-194.

Paterson, Isabel. "Rue with a Difference," *Books,* V (August 4, 1929), 1.

Richardson, Eudora Ramsey. "Richmond and Its Writers," *Bookman,* LXVIII (December, 1928), 450-451.

Rogers, Cameron. "Realism from the Romantic South," *World's Work,* L (May, 1925), 99-102.

Van Gelder, Robert. "An Interview with Miss Ellen Glasgow," *New York Times Book Review,* October 18, 1942, 2.

Wilson, James S. "Ellen Glasgow: 1941," *Virginia Quarterly Review,* XVII (Winter, 1941), 317-320.

"Ellen Glasgow: Ironic Idealist," *Virginia Quarterly Review,* XV (January, 1939), 121-126.

"Ellen Glasgow's Novels," *Virginia Quarterly Review,* IX (October, 1933), 595-600.

"Two American Novels," *Virginia Quarterly Review,* XI (October, 1935), 620-625.

Young, Stark. "Prefaces of Distinction," *New Republic,* LXXV (June 7, 1933), 101-102.

*Contains biographical material.

WILLA CATHER

A native of Winchester, Virginia, Willa Sibert Cather (1876-1947) spent her youth in Nebraska, where her father owned a ranch. Until of high school age, she studied at home with her grandmother, reading extensively in the English and Latin classics. She graduated from the University of Nebraska at nineteen, and shortly afterwards went to Pittsburgh, so that she might hear good music and follow through with the newspaper writing by which she had earned her way in college. But work as telegraph editor and dramatic critic for the *Pittsburgh Daily Ledger* failed to interest her more than a few years; in 1901 she tried high school teaching.

Meanwhile, numerous short stories from her pen had appeared in magazines, with the result that *McClure's* offered her an editorship. After resigning from this position, Miss Cather devoted herself to free-lance writing.

The novels of Willa Cather have been translated into several foreign languages, notably the Scandinavian tongues and Czech. Five universities conferred upon her the honorary doctorate, Michigan, Nebraska, Columbia, Yale, and Princeton. The Pulitzer Prize came to Miss Cather in 1922 for *One of Ours*, and in 1933 she received the *Prix Femina Americaine*. She was also awarded the gold medal of the National Institute of Arts and Letters.

THE NOVELS:

Alexander's Bridge. Boston and New York: Houghton Mifflin, 1912.

O Pioneers! Boston and New York: Houghton Mifflin, 1913.

The Song of the Lark. Boston and New York: Houghton Mifflin, 1915.

My Antonia. Boston and New York: Houghton Mifflin, 1918.

One of Ours. New York: Alfred A. Knopf, 1922.

A Lost Lady. New York. Alfred A. Knopf, 1923.

The Professor's House. New York: Alfred A. Knopf, 1925.

My Mortal Enemy. New York: Alfred A. Knopf, 1926.

Death Comes for the Archbishop. New York: Alfred A. Knopf, 1927.

Shadows on the Rock. New York: Alfred A. Knopf, 1931.

Lucy Gayheart. New York: Alfred A. Knopf, 1935.

Sapphira and the Slave Girl. New York: Alfred A. Knopf, 1940.

CRITICAL:

Not Under Forty, New York: Alfred A. Knopf, 1936.

"The Novel Demeublé," *New Republic,* XXX, Pt. 2, (April 12, 1922), 5-6.

ABOUT THE AUTHOR:

*Bénet, Stephen Vincent and Rosemary. "Willa Cather: Civilized and very American," *Books,* XVII (December 15, 1940), 6.

*Bogan, Louise. "American Classic," *New Yorker,* VII (August 8, 1931), 19-22).

Boynton, P. H. *Some Contemporary Americans.* Chicago: University Press, 1924.

Canby, H. S. "Willa Cather: A Reminiscence," *Saturday Review of Literature,* XXX (May, 1947), 22-24.

Carroll, Latrobe. "Willa Sibert Cather," *Bookman,* LIV (May 1, 1921), 212-214.

Fadiman, Clifton. "Willa Cather, the Past Recaptured," *Nation,* CXXXV (December 7, 1932), 564-565.

Footman, H. H. "The Genius of Willa Cather," *American Literature*, X (May, 1938), 123-141.

Hicks, Granville. "The Case against Willa Cather," *English Journal*, XXII (November, 1933), 703-710.

Jones, H. M. "The Novels of Willa Cather," *Saturday Review of Literature*, XVIII (August 6, 1938), 3-4.

Kronenberger, Louis. "Willa Cather," *Bookman*, LXXIV (October, 1931), 134-140.

*Kunitz, Stanley J. and Haycraft, Howard. *Twentieth Century Authors*. New York: H. H. Wilson, 1942.

McNamara, Robert. "Phases of American Religion in Thornton Wilder and Willa Cather," *Catholic World*, CXXXV (September, 1932), 641-649.

Meyers, W. L. "The Novel Dedicate," *Virginia Quarterly Review*, VIII (July, 1932), 410-418.

*Millet, Fred B. *Contemporary American Authors*. New York: Harcourt, Brace, 1940.

Monroe, N. Elizabeth. *The Novel and Society*. Chapel Hill, N. C. University Press, 1941.

Morris, Lloyd. "Willa Cather," *North American Review*, CCXIX (May, 1924), 641-652.

*Overton, Grant. *The Women Who Make Our Novels*. New York: Moffatt, Yard, 1918.

Rapin, René. *Willa Cather*. New York. McBride, 1930.

*Sergeant, Elizabeth Shipley. "Willa Cather, Work and Personality," *New Republic*, XLIII (June 17, 1925), 91.

Trilling, Lionel. "Willa Cather," *New Republic*, LXX (February 10, 1937), 10-13.

Whipple, T. K. *Spokesmen*. New York and London: D. Appleton, 1928.

White, G. L., Jr. "Willa Cather," *Sewanee Review*, L (January, 1942), 18-25.

Wilson, James S. "Shadows on the Rock," *Virginia Quarterly Review*, VII (October, 1931), 585-590.

"Two American Novels," *Virginia Quarterly Review*, XI (October, 1935), 620-625.

Winsten, Archer. "A Defense of Willa Cather," *Bookman*, LXXIV (March, 1932), 634-640.

*Contains biographical material.